HITLER'S TEUTONIC KNIGHTS

SS Panzers in action

HITLER'S TEUTONIC KNIGHTS

SS Panzers in action

BRUCE QUARRIE

Patrick Stephens, Wellingborough

Dedication
This book is for two people—Bill Sharpe for teaching me
how to write and Terry Gander for teaching me how to
do historical research into military subjects. Any faults in
it are mine, not theirs.

First published in March 1986
Revised edition 1989

British Library Cataloguing in Publication Data

Quarrie, Bruce
    Hitler's Teutonic Knights
    1. Waffenschutzstaffel—History. 2. Germany,
    Heer—Armoured troops 3. World War, 1939-1945
    —Tank warfare
    I. Title
    355'.00943   D757.54

    ISBN 0-85059-764-1

Patrick Stephens Limited is part of
the Thorsons Publishing Group,
Wellingborough, Northamptonshire,
NN8 2RQ, England

Printed in Great Britain by
Butler & Tanner Limited,
Frome, Somerset

10 9 8 7 6 5 4 3 2 1

Front endpapers Das Reich *Tiger and grenadiers during
the battle of Kursk* (BA 81/143/12A).

Half title *The German eagle presides over the Sigrunes and
the SS motto* (BA 81/141/36).

Title spread *PzKpfw Vs of* Das Reich *advance across the
Russian steppe* (BA 73/96/62).

Page 6 *Tiger in war-torn Budapest, 1945* (BA
680/8282a/32a).

Contents

Introduction

History, a writer more famous than myself once said, 'is merely propaganda written by the victors'. As far as the Waffen-SS is concerned, this is more than usually true. This body of fighting men has, however, had its case fairly put before the public in Gerald Reitlinger's *The SS: Alibi of a nation*, which was first published in 1956. Reitlinger's book showed that the SS as a whole was not only regarded by the victorious Allies as the prime perpetrator of civil and military crimes, but was used by the remainder of the German population as a convenient scapegoat as well.

Controversy continued to rage nevertheless until, in 1983, Patrick Stephens published my earlier book, *Hitler's Samurai*. In this I attempted to prove—and no one has yet contradicted me—that the Waffen-SS obeyed the warrior code of the Japanese samurai, transmitted via the mechanism of the Jesuit organization and Himmler's imagination into twentieth-century practice. In this book I also attempted to show that there are always two sides to a coin: that the Waffen-SS was culpable of war atrocities and of involvement in the running of the concentration camps; but that at the same time it was capable not just of chivalry, but also of conducting some of the most brilliant campaigns of the Second World War, and of influencing the outcome of the latter to no insignificant degree.

The book has sold well, for which I am grateful to my readers, although I am far from becoming a Len Deighton! It also provoked a large volume of correspondence and telephone calls, some complimentary and some—mostly from those who appear to have seen it but not read it—quite vituperative.

With these exceptions, *Hitler's Samurai* has received a generally warm response and a demand for 'more', in particular for more photographs and for more details about the operations of the premier Waffen-SS divisions: the Panzer divisions. This book has been written purely as a result of that call. It deals principally with the operational histories of the seven true SS Panzer divisions. I make no apologies for the differing lengths of the chapters. The Leibstandarte *Adolf Hitler* was first, and its history deserves the greatest coverage. *Das Reich* was second, and this is similarly reflected. *Totenkopf* was third in name but lower than that in status. *Wiking*, the first 'European' unit, has a combat record bettered by none. *Hohenstaufen* and *Frundsberg* were raised late in the war and, although they fought well, did not significantly alter its outcome. *Hitlerjugend*, the last of the seven, and last raised, did. I have accorded each its appropriate number of pages.

One factor which has influenced the composition of this book has been the availability of photographs. *Das Reich* and *Totenkopf* predominate, and there is a good reason for this. Most of the pictures come from the Bundesarchiv in Koblenz. Their fund of some one and half million photographs is what remains of over twice that number taken by Kriegsberichter (see Appendix 1) during the war. A similar number 'disappeared' in 1945 and these were either destroyed or are in Soviet hands. Many more were 'lifted' while the negatives were stored in Washington between the end of the war and their return to the West German government. Personally, I refuse to purchase 'unpublished' photographs from private individuals who have no right to them.

I also beg your indulgence in another respect. *Hitler's Samurai* has received some criticism because of its title rather than because of its content. I admit, it was an eyecatching title but, like many, it did not come until the book was virtually completed. It is still apt and its explanation will be found on pages 26-27. When I was asked to write a sequel, concentrating on the SS Panzer divisions, I was for a long time stuck for a title until I came across the following passage from my friend Ian Heath's book, *The Crusades*.

'The sinister reputation of the Teutonic Knights...resulted not from their brief Levantine career but rather from their infamous activities in Prussia, Lithuania and Poland...The Order was actually founded in Outremer in 1190 when, during the Third Crusade, merchants of Bremen and Lübeck established a hospital for the care of German pilgrims at the siege of Acre. It turned military in 1198 when many German knights joined following the abortive German crusade of 1197. The Order went under a variety of names until 1220, when it adopted its full title of the Hospital of St Mary of the House of Teutons of Jerusalem. It was always exclusively German-speaking and, except for Romania, the Baltic lands and (briefly) Hungary, outside of Outremer it held estates only in Germany itself.

'Officially, the Order's headquarters was always at Acre, despite the fact that the Templars drove them out of the city on one occasion, but their chief stronghold from 1229 until 1271 was actually Montfort, which they renamed Starkenberg. However, in Syria the Order was always very much overshadowed by the Temple and the Hospital, and it instead concentrated most of its attentions in the Levant on enterprises in Cilicia, where the main fortresses amongst its many possessions were Adamodana and Harunia. Even so, Teutonic contingents were present at most major engagements of the 13th century, including Bahr Ashmun (1221), La Forbie (1244) and El Mansurah (1250). Fifteen brethren were present at the fall of Acre in 1291, of whom only the Order's *Hochmeister* or Grand Master escaped alive. The Order thereafter transferred its headquarters to Venice before moving on to Marienburg in Prussia in 1308.

'Like the Templars and Hospitallers, the Teutonic Knights employed large numbers of Turcopoles, these probably supplying the bulk of the allegedly 300-strong Teutonic contingent at La Forbie and certainly comprising the greatest part of Starkenberg's garrison at its fall in 1271. They also had brother sergeants, confrère brethren (called *Halbbruders*), mercenaries and the vassals of the Order's estates.'

If this sounds like a description of an early version of the Waffen-SS, it is not surprising, and anyone who has seen Eisenstein's brilliant film *Alexander Nevsky* can appreciate the parallel even more closely. Swap mounted knights in armour charging across a frozen lake for Panzers roaring across exactly the same landscape, and what other title could I have chosen for this book?

Bruce Quarrie
Wellingborough, 1987

Right *Hitler watching the* Deutschland *Regiment on manoeuvres at Munsterlager in the summer of 1938. Next to him are Himmler and SS-Gruppenführer Karl Wolff. Paul Hausser is on the extreme left of the picture* (BPK/NS-Zeit).

1. 1st SS Panzer Division Leibstandarte *Adolf Hitler*

Clear the streets, the SS marches,
The storm-columns stand at the ready.
They will take the road
From tyranny to freedom.
So we are all ready to give our all
As did our fathers before us.
Let death be our battle companion.
We are the black band.

So sang the men of the Leibstandarte SS *Adolf Hitler* (LSS*AH*), first—though not always foremost—of the Waffen-SS legions as they marched through Berlin under the light of tens of thousands of burning pitch and resin torches, beneath the translucently fluttering red, white and black flags, on that evening of Adolf Hitler's appointment as Chancellor of Germany. They had come a long way in ten short years, this 'black band', since they had first been raised in March 1923 as a group of a mere 200 men, known simply as the Adolf Hitler Stosstruppe, dedicated to preserving the life of one man—Adolf Hitler. The SS now numbered 52,000, still only a sixth of the number of Röhm's brown-uniformed SA, or Sturmabteilung (stormtroopers), but Himmler and Dietrich's creation would soon dispose of the latter and grow to triple the SA's original strength. Even then, for all its military prowess, the Waffen-SS never became the threat feared by the Army and, despite its achievements, and the encouragement in its growth awarded by Hitler after the winter battles of 1941 and 1942, never grew to exceed ten per cent of the Army's strength.

Of all the SS Divisions, the Leibstandarte *Adolf Hitler* ('Leibstandarte' meaning bodyguard; it is frequently printed as 'Liebstandarte', which means something entirely different. . .) is most usually held up by historians as the principal SS formation. In number and in name, this is true. Whether, on the battlefield, it is really true I leave to the reader to judge. From a personal point of view I would accord this honour to either *Das Reich* or *Wiking*. But we are leaping ahead of our story, for in 1933 the Waffen-SS as such did not exist, while the creation of SS Panzer divisions lay even further in the future.

The SS itself was primarily the creation of a scrawny, balding, bespectacled son of a rigid and pedantic Munich schoolmaster: Heinrich Himmler. Unprepossessing in appearance, cold and authoritarian in manner, yet with the imagination of a man to whom books and ancient legends were more 'real' than life itself, he was a strange adjunct to the man who would alter European history more than any single individual since Napoleon. Himmler assumed control of the SS (Schutzstaffel) in January 1929. It had originally been formed by an uneducated bully named Joseph ('Sepp') Dietrich to protect Hitler during the time of the attempted Munich putsch in 1923 which resulted in Hitler being consigned to prison (during this period he finished writing *Mein Kampf*) and the SA being declared illegal. Being so tiny, the fledgling SS was overlooked by the

Right *Himmler adresses the Leibstandarte at the end of the French campaign, Metz, 1940. The standard is held by Oberstumführer Heinrich Springer* (Christopher Ailsby Photographic Collection).

Leibstandarte Adolf Hitler

Left *Photographs of SS troops in action during the Polish campaign are extremely rare. This shows a machine-gun team in a foxhole and is reproduced from a German book entitled* Die Wehrmacht 1940 *in my possession which contains chapters relating, from the 'official' viewpoint, the events of 1939-40. Of interest is the SS camouflage tunic which was ridiculed by the Army at this time.*

Left *Another photograph from the same source showing SS grenadiers assisting a wounded comrade to safety. Enthusiasts will share my own delight in the clarity of equipment detail.*

authorities and its organization was taken over by Julius Schreck —a man virtually unrecognized in the history books, but one who had an unparalleled effect on the SS's eventual character and motivation.

As Gerald Reitlinger* so rightly says, Hitler is the best commentator on the SS at that time.

'Being convinced that there are always circumstances in which élite troops are called for, I created in 1922-3 the "Adolf Hitler Shock Troops". They were made up of men who were ready for revolution and knew that some day things would come to hard knocks.'

The 'knocks' that the Waffen-SS was to receive, as well as to deliver, were at that time, of course, unthought of.

Schreck, who became Hitler's chauffeur after his release from Landsberg prison, formulated the ground rules for admission into the SS which were later to be polished and refined by Himmler. There were age limits—23 to 35—which eliminated teenage ruffians and ensured that members were at the peak of their potential physical health; applicants had to have two recognized sponsors, and a police certificate stating that they had not been in trouble for the last five years. Alcoholics were also excluded. These ideals fell far short of the racial and physical standards which would be demanded later for admission to the Leibstandarte, but they were a start. However, Schreck gave up the unequal struggle with the Sturmabteilung 'brownshirts' after only a couple of years of infighting, and his place was taken in 1926 by Joseph Berchtold, an NSDAP treasury official. He, too, proved unequal to the task and, on 6 January 1929, the weak-chinned but fanatically determined Heinrich Himmler took over the helm. The SA was delighted, because they thought him weak and controllable. How wrong they were!

Utilizing Hitler's incipient paranoia to the full, Himmler concocted assassination plots which convinced the Führer that he needed a personal bodyguard which would be loyal only to himself, and completely separate from the SA 'monster' which he had created but could not control. The story of the Röhm putsch is well known. In one fell swoop, known ever afterwards as 'the night of the long knives', the SA was beheaded and the SS, as

*The SS: Alibi of a Nation 1922-1945 (Heinemann, 1956).

Himmler planned, became the real power behind the throne. The Leibstandarte *Adolf Hitler* had achieved its first 'military' success.

The growth of the SS in general and the political difficulties which hindered the progress of the Waffen-SS in particular until at least 1942 are discussed in detail in my earlier book, *Hitler's Samurai*. Through all these difficulties, however, the Leibstandarte *Adolf Hitler* survived and blossomed. In 1936 the growing cadre of black-uniformed soldiers was to the fore when Germany re-occupied the Sudetenland; in 1938 they marched into Austria, and in 1939 into Czechoslovakia. Then came Poland, and the first proper taste of action.

The Leibstandarte *Adolf Hitler*, its ranks now swelled to 3,700 men in four infantry battalions with supporting artillery, anti-tank, pioneer and reconnaissance units, was attached to von Rundstedt's 10th Army as part of Army Group South. Its first battle honours were gained when it stormed the positions of the Polish 10th Infantry Division across the River Prosna; it then faced a suicidal counter-attack, First World War-style, with cavalry and sabres, outside Boleslavecz. In the fierce hand-to-hand fighting which ensued, the Leibstandarte *Adolf Hitler* showed that ferocious fighting spirit which characterized all operations of the élite SS units—and won. Around Pabianice they encountered both heavy artillery and snipers. The Army's 23rd Panzer Regiment had abandoned its attempt to crack this particular nut, so it was up to the SS, wading through chest-high maize, to demolish the determined defence. They marched on, capturing Oltarzev and Blonie on their way to Warsaw. They were ruthless—and they were responsible for the first recorded atrocity by the armed SS in World War 2 when part of their artillery company massacred fifty Jews who had been herded into a synagogue. The repercussions of this were widespread. The Army insisted that the men responsible be tried by courts martial; Himmler prevailed upon Hitler to grant his men freedom from Wehrmacht jurisdiction, and they went unpunished. This served merely to aggravate the suspicion and dislike with which the Waffen-SS was regarded by the Army.

Following the invasion of Poland, Britain and France had declared a state of war between themselves and Germany, but for nine months, apart from border incidents, naval skirmishes and aerial dogfights, little occurred. This was the period of the so-called 'phoney war', when both sides girded themselves for the struggle to follow. The Leibstandarte *Adolf Hitler* was expanded and fully equipped as a genuine motorized infantry regiment. It had already shed its black uniform for the Polish campaign and, in common with the SS-VT (see Chapters 2 and 3), was now garbed in grey, with silver SS runes on black collar patches. Moreover, the regiment was, uniquely among the SS at this time, equipped with a contingent of PzKpfw IV tanks. They were, as Gerald Reitlinger describes them, a 'show force', and were both envied and resented by the remainder of the SS-VT and *Totenkopf* troops. They were deliberately assigned 'glamorous' tasks by Hitler.

First came the invasion of Holland where the Leibstandarte, together with the *Der Führer* Regiment of the SS-VT, was scheduled to take part in the triumphant capture of Amsterdam. Crossing the border near De Poppe, an assault detachment neatly disposed of the unfortunate Dutch frontier guards together with the demolition charges which had been placed to destroy the bridge, and opened the barriers for the long column of tanks and other vehicles which then poured through, supported from overhead by waves of Ju 52 transport aircraft carrying Fallschirmjäger and Ju 87 'Stuka' dive bombers—the aerial artillery of blitzkrieg. Pushing rapidly on, the LSS*AH* covered fifty miles (eighty km) in the first six hours of the campaign, only to find that the Dutch defenders *had* succeeded in demolishing their first objective, the bridge at Zwolle. Undeterred, the SS improvized rafts from materials ripped from nearby farms and forced a crossing of the River Yssel, took the town of Hooen with 200 prisoners and pushed forward nearly another fifty miles. This resulted in the much publicized first Iron Cross of the campaign, awarded to Obersturmführer Hugo Krass of the regiment's 3rd Battalion.

However, the Dutch destruction of the Yssel bridge interrupted the main German thrust towards Amsterdam, and the 'show force' was therefore switched to join 9th Panzer Division and the rest of the SS-VT which had thundered westwards towards the Moerdijk bridges on the approach to Rotterdam —and *these* bridges had been captured by German Fallschirmjäger.

Whatever happened later in the war, the bombing raid which devastated Rotterdam and brought forth worldwide condemnation of Nazi Germany was a mistake. Lack of communication between ground and air meant that the pilots of the Heinkel He 111s did not realize that the city had all but fallen; only a few received the recall order; and Rotterdam was pulverized. The stunned Dutch government capitulated and this part of the 1940 campaign would have been over but for one strange incident: Luftwaffe General Kurt Student, founding father of the German parachute forces, was wounded and nearly killed by men of the LSSAH who—not realizing that Holland had surrendered—opened fire on a group of Dutch soldiers. As it turned out, they had justification. The Dutch government might have surrendered, but the Army had not. As the Leibstandarte pushed on through Rotterdam towards The Hague, it encountered heavy rifle and machine-gun fire in Delft.

The regiment was now moved south towards Arras where, on 21 May, British and French tanks had administered a sharp check to both Rommel's 7th Panzer Division and *Totenkopf*. On the 24th, the Leibstandarte was in position by the Aa Canal, on the south-eastern flank of beleaguered Dunkirk. At this point the German forces received their ludicrous 'halt' order from Hitler, who had become convinced that things were going so well, something must be wrong! Whatever, the Leibstandarte was in position and 'Sepp' Dietrich was never one to follow orders he disbelieved in, even when they came from his old friend Hitler. The attack went forward as originally planned, the regiment crossing the canal and seizing the Watten heights. Perhaps spurred on by this and other successes, Hitler belatedly gave permission for the advance to continue—but too late to prevent the escape of the bulk of the British Expeditionary Force in the magnificent saga of 'the small boats'. Unfortunately, this stage of the campaign was to involve the LSS*AH* in one of the first of the gross atrocities for which the whole SS would shoulder the blame in post-war years.

Above right *A Leibstandarte SdKfz 231 with its turret trained to the rear prepares to haul away a fallen tree — either clearing or setting up a road block* (BPK WII103).

Right *A Leibstandarte StuG III in France. Note the crewman is wearing the field-grey self-propelled gun crew version of the SS Panzer jacket* (BPK WII103 2514).

'Sepp' Dietrich (in shirtsleeves) at a field briefing of Leibstandarte officers during the 1940 campaign (BA 81/141/13).

A small and unimportant town in the path of the Leibstandarte's advance, Wormhoudt lies some twelve miles (nineteen km) from Dunkirk. 'Sepp' Dietrich very nearly did not live to see it. His car came under heavy fire and burst into flames, while he threw himself into a culvert for safety, covering himself with wet mud to avoid the heat of the flames. He was to lie there for five hours while elements of his regiment fought to extricate him under a hail of fire from a strongly defended British position. Meanwhile, the rest of the regiment, incensed by the thought that their commander had—as they believed—been killed, advanced upon Wormhoudt, which was defended by 331 men of the 2nd Royal Warwickshire Regiment, the Cheshire Regiment and the Royal Artillery. They fought hard but were ultimately defeated by a combination of Luftwaffe bombing and Leibstandarte fanaticism. Unfortunately, some eighty men were taken prisoner by the 7th Company of the Leibstandarte's 2nd Battalion—whose commander, Sturmbannführer Schutzek, had been badly wounded in the attack.

The prisoners were marched into a barn—they thought at the time that it was for shelter from the rain which had begun to fall. Their only officer, Captain Lynn-Allen, complained to the guards that there was not enough room for all his wounded to lie down. An infuriated guard, whose name has never been revealed, threw a hand grenade into the packed barn. Lynn-Allen, together with Private Bert Evans, made a dash for freedom. Both were shot by the guard, Lynn-Allen fatally. Bert Evans, badly wounded, feigned death and the guard walked away. Evans listened, helpless, to the sound of further shots, grenade explosions and screams, as the remainder of the prisoners were slaughtered. Fifteen

Himmler congratulates Dietrich on the Leibstandarte's performance at the successful conclusion of the French campaign (BPK WII 8574).

men, including Evans, survived, most volunteering to enter captivity rather than risk reprisals on the local civilian population. When their story came out after the war it was, like that of the Le Paradis massacre (see Chapter 3), received with incredulity. None of the culprits was ever brought to justice. The Leibstandarte looks after its own.

Shortly afterwards, the Leibstandarte was pulled back to Cambrai to rest for a couple of days before the offensive was renewed into France. Attached to von Kleist's Panzergruppe, the SS encountered surprisingly strong resistance and the Germans pulled back to try an attack on another part of the line. Again the Leibstandarte was detached, however, this time to 44th Army Korps which was rapidly advancing towards the River Marne. By this time (10 June) French resistance was rapidly crumbling and the advance became headlong, with the Leibstandarte in the lead as often as not. On to Moulins, where the French demolished the road bridge over the River Allier but left the railway bridge intact, even though on fire; on to Pourcain, then to St Etienne, which was reached on 24 June. On the very next day a cease-fire was declared and the Leibstandarte halted, having achieved the deepest penetration into France of any German unit. 'Sepp' Dietrich and his men were moved to Metz at the end of the campaign, where no doubt they enjoyed a mighty celebration.

Hitler was delighted with the performance of the regiment and, on 6 August, authorized its expansion to the size of a brigade. The next few months were quiet, but in October Italy invaded Greece and it soon became apparent that, while the Italian Army might be fine for fighting Ethiopian tribesmen, it was no match for the tough Greeks. Reluctantly, since he had originally planned to invade Russia in

Pre-war photograph of the Leibstandarte on parade. Munich, 9 November 1935. In the foreground is Theodor Wisch.

the spring of 1941, Hitler decided that he had to help his ally. The Leibstandarte entrained from Metz in February, being attached to Wilhelm List's 12th Army along with the *Grossdeutschland* and their comrades-in-arms from Holland, the 9th Panzer Division. Attacking via Bulgaria and Yugoslavia, the Leibstandarte achieved a notable success in only three days by capturing the Greek stronghold of Monastir.

The next task was more difficult. The Klidi Pass, which had to be captured, was defended by Australians and New Zealanders of the Empire Expeditionary Force which had been rushed to Greece as quickly as possible after the Italian invasion. However, the Leibstandarte succeeded, though at a cost of over fifty dead and 150 wounded. What followed is one of the most celebrated incidents in the Leibstandarte's history: it features in Kurt 'Panzer' Meyer's autobiography, *Grenadiere*, and was a story he loved to recount at post-war reunions. Meyer at this time was commander of the Leibstandarte's reconnaissance battalion, which had been entrusted with the seizure of the Klissura Pass. This was heavily defended by Greek soldiers well dug-in with machine-guns and demolition charges, and for once the SS soldiers were disheartened, diving for cover behind rocks and in shell craters.

Meyer recalls: 'We glue ourselves behind rocks and dare not move. A feeling of nausea tightens my throat. I yell to [Untersturmführer] Emil Wawrzinek to get the attack moving. But the good Emil just looks at me as if he has doubts about my sanity. Machine-gun fire smacks against the rocks in front of us. . . How I can get Wawrzinek to take that first leap? In my distress, I feel the smooth roundness of an egg hand grenade in my hand. I shout at the group. Everybody looks thunderstruck at me as I brandish the hand grenade, pull the pin, and roll it precisely behind the last man. Never again did I witness such a concerted leap forward as at that second. As if bitten by tarantulas, we dive around the rock spur and into a fresh crater. The spell is broken. The hand grenade has cured our lameness. We grin at each other, and head forward toward the next cover.'

The pass was duly taken and Meyer was awarded the Knight's Cross. The rest of the Greek campaign was easier and the Leibstandarte took enormous numbers of prisoners as the Greek resistance gradually crumbled. Meyer's battalion alone captured 11,000 the day after the assault on the Klissura Pass, and the brigade took the surrender of no fewer than sixteen divisions three days before the Greek government capitulated. It then chased the retreating

Empire Expeditionary Force across the Corinth Canal, which German paratroops had tried, and only narrowly failed, to capture in advance of the Allied retreat. However, as at Dunkirk, the Allies were evacuated by sea, to Crete, and the Leibstandarte entrained for Prague prior to the invasion of Russia.

Enlarged to the size of a full motorized infantry division, the Leibstandarte was attached to Army Group South under Feldmarschal Gerd von Rundstedt. From its start line at Lublin, in Poland, the LSS*AH,* 10,796-strong, headed rapidly towards the River Vistula, aiming for Galicia and the western Ukraine. The brigade smashed through the Stalin Line like the proverbial knife through butter, but then received a shock at Romanovka when it encountered Soviet T-34 tanks for the first time. Rupert Butler* describes the scene graphically.

'Here was something that could not be kicked,

whipped, bullied or machine-gunned. This magnificent piece of armour was immune except to the 88 mm flak gun. The Soviet assaults came in continuous waves against the thin SS formations. . .

'The attacks came hourly and the men of the Leibstandarte noticed that the troops seemed to be of an altogether higher calibre, at least in terms of violent courage, than the Germans had encountered previously. Charges were made with the bayonet and engagements were hand-to-hand. In country of deep forest, Germans and Russians hacked and stabbed at one another, while mortars burst their lethal shrapnel.'

Aerial support was finally called up and the Russian counter-attack dispersed. While the *Wiking*

The Black Angels (Hamlyn, 1978).

The Leibstandarte's key device on the back of a truck (BA 73/99/70).

Division was mopping up in Zhitomir, the Leibstandarte pressed on towards Kiev. Together with *Wiking* it was then detached to help the 11th and 17th Armies which were hard pressed at Uman. The two SS divisions completed an encirclement of three Russian Armies, one of many such successes during the early part of Operation 'Barbarossa'. 100,000 Soviet soldiers were taken prisoner. Generalmajor Werner Kempf, the Korps commander, had nothing but praise for the Leibstandarte.

'Since 24 July, the Leibstandarte SS *Adolf Hitler* has taken the most glorious part in the encirclement of the enemy around Uman. Committed at the focus of the battle for the seizure of the key enemy positions at Archangelsk, the Leibstandarte SS *Adolf Hitler*, with incomparable dash, took the city and the heights to the south. In the spirit of the most devoted brotherhood of arms, they intervened on their own initiative in the arduous struggle of the 16th Infantry Division (motorized) on their left flank and routed the enemy, destroying numerous tanks.'

In fact, the Leibstandarte destroyed 64 tanks and took 2,200 prisoners.

Then it was on to Taganrog, across the River Msus, and here the full brutality of the Russian campaign was forced home upon the SS men. Six Leibstandarte soldiers had been captured by the Russians. After being tortured, they were hacked to pieces with axes and bayonets and their mutilated bodies dumped in a well, where their comrades found them. In a towering rage, 'Sepp' Dietrich ordered that all prisoners taken over the next three days were to be shot out of hand.

As November arrived, and with it snow, the Leibstandarte was braced for the assault upon Rostov-on-Don. They had advanced a thousand miles (1,600 km) in just over four months. And they were about to face their first defeat. Rostov was very heavily defended, and after eight days of intense street fighting, the division could do no more. Gerd von Rundstedt, one of the German Army's most skilled and respected soldiers, sent a message to Hitler saying that a retreat behind the lines of the River Msus was essential. After the war, he said: 'An order came to me from the Führer: "Remain where you are and retreat no further". I immediately wired back: "It is madness to attempt to hold. In the first place the troops cannot do it, and in the second place if they do not retreat they will be destroyed. I repeat that this

order be rescinded or that you find someone else." That same night the Führer's reply arrived: "I am acceding to your request. Please give up your command."' However, von Rundstedt had already ordered his men to retreat, and they dug in to await the winter and the expected Russian counter-offensive.

The Leibstandarte, *Wiking* and other weary, cold German formations in the Donets region held out, as described in Chapter 4. Then, in the spring came a renewal of hope, and the Leibstandarte participated in a successful operation to cut off a Russian salient at Kharkov before, thankfully, returning to France where the division was to be brought back up to strength and be re-equipped as a fully fledged Panzergrenadier formation, between August and November. It then did occupation duty in Toulon until the end of the year before returning to the east, together with *Das Reich* and *Totenkopf*, which had been similarly equipped with a tank regiment apiece and armoured half-tracks instead of trucks for the infantry regiments.

Following the disaster of Stalingrad, there were grave fears of a repetition in Kharkov at the beginning of 1943. Paul Hausser, in command of the new SS Panzer Korps comprising the Leibstandarte *Adolf Hitler, Das Reich* and *Totenkopf*, was entrusted with the task of ensuring that there was not. CO of Army Group Don had already taken the unprecedented step of flying to see Hitler in order to plead with him to permit a retreat west of Kharkov. This time, Hitler grudgingly acceded, but to a general withdrawal only. The troops in Kharkov, he insisted, were not under Manstein's command (they principally consisted of the independent Kampfgruppe Lanz) and must remain. When Hausser arrived in advance of his new Panzer Korps, to assess the situation, he saw immediately that such a course was not only desperate but criminally stupid. He wired an urgent memo to his Führer:

'Inside Kharkov mob firing at troops and vehicles. No forces available for mopping-up since everything in front line. City, including railway, stores and ammunition dumps, effectively dynamited at Army

Above right *Flamethrower team in action against a French strongpoint.*
Right *Victory parade through Paris* (BPK WII60 F 3708b & WII63 F 3920a).

A motor cycle team already covered with the dust of conquest, France, May 1940 (BPK WII101 F 3925a).

Left *Soviet tank crew surrender to an SS grenadier* (BPK WII131 F 3623b).

Above *Leibstandarte PzKpfw IV knocked out during the heavy fighting for Kharkov in March 1943* (BA 330/3021/21a).

Below *Leibstandarte PzKpfw IIs and IIIs in Kharkov* (BA 73/113/10).

Hitler's Teutonic Knights

Left *Leibstandarte Tiger and PzKpfw IV outside Kharkov* (BA 277/843/14).

Below left *A tiny LSSAH badge can just be seen on the extreme top left-hand hull rear of this PzKpfw IV, accompanied by grenadiers, in Kharkov* (BA 73/113/15).

Below *Men of the Leibstandarte manhandle a 7.5 cm Pak 40 into action in Kharkov* (BA 73/84/55).

Right *An officer of the Leibstandarte in Kharkov, wearing the 'old style' cap without cords and the parka which was issued to Waffen-SS units at around this time* (BA 330/3021/27a).

Below right *Leibstandarte PzKpfw IVF2 outside Kharkov* (BA 73/85/74).

orders. City burning. Systematic withdrawal increasingly improbable each day. Assumptions underlying Kharkov's strategic importance no longer valid. Request renewed Führer decision whether Kharkov to be defended to the last man.'

Hitler's reply was curt and to the point:

'1. The eastern front of Kharkov must be held.
'2. The considerable SS formations now arriving must be employed in freeing Kharkov's communications and in defeating the enemy forces pressing against Kharkov from the north-west.'

Hausser sent in *Das Reich* but withheld his other two divisions. This rapidly proved the hopelessness of the situation and the division was enmeshed in deadly street fighting against grossly superior forces. Führer directive or not, Hausser took a unilateral decision to retire. He pulled *Das Reich* out—just in time, as it turned out—and withdrew his Korps to Krasnograd, intending to lure the Russians into a trap. Hitler was white-lipped with fury but miraculously did not recall Hausser, for now the SS Panzer Korps was to show just what it could achieve when handed a militarily secure rather than suicidal position.

Together with the Army's 48th Panzer Korps, Hausser launched his counter-attack on 19 February 1943. The Russians, who had sensed complete victory within their grasp, reeled back in disorder at the ferocity and skill of the assault. An entire Soviet corps was encircled by Hausser's three divisions and wiped out. The Russians, as Rupert Butler so aptly describes the situation, were behaving like 'demented lemmings', throwing forces into the battle with no thought for strategy whatsoever. Their 25th Guards Rifle Division flung itself against Hausser's tanks. For five days they exhausted themselves, and the weather was gradually improving, which was in the Germans' favour.

Now Hausser issued his orders to his divisional commanders, 'Sepp' Dietrich, Ernst Vahl (deputizing for Georg Keppler) and Max Simon, who had taken over from Theodor Eicke following his death in an air crash only a few days before. On 11 March the Leibstandarte entered the city with *Das Reich* on its left and *Totenkopf* on the right. At the end of the battle, when the Russian losses during February and March were totalled, they came to 52 divisions and brigades. Hitler was jubilant and called Goebbels in

to celebrate. The Reich Propaganda Minister later wrote: 'He was exceptionally happy about the way the SS Leibstandarte was led by "Sepp" Dietrich. This man personally performed real deeds of heroism and has proved himself a great strategist in conducting his operations.'

'The SS Panzer Korps,' declared Hitler, 'is worth twenty Italian divisions.'

Now came the build-up for the momentous battle of Kursk, in many respects the central turning point of the war. The SS divisions were issued with new tanks—Tigers and Panthers—to make good their losses during the battle for Kharkov. The Kursk salient was the most outstanding feature of the front line in Russia as spring gradually turned to summer. The German General Staff was not long in coming to the conclusion that a successful summer 1943 offensive aimed—at long last—at capturing Moscow, could not be launched without first 'pinching off' this ulcer in their flank. Plans were therefore put in hand for a two-pronged encirclement on a narrow front from both north and south, in which it was hoped the Soviet forces around Kursk would be trapped.

However, the Russians were equally quick to see the vital importance of their positions here, and began reinforcing them heavily at the same time as the Germans were commencing their own build-up. Marshal Zhukov recommended a strong defence in depth against which the German forces would wear themselves down, followed by a counter-attack when

they were suitably exhausted. This plan was criticized in some quarters since it was felt wrong to hand the Germans the initiative on a plate, while others felt strongly that attack was still the best means of defence. Tactically, the Marshal was to be proved wrong, but other political and strategic factors were to come into play and ultimately vindicate him.

South of Kursk, where the main effort was to be concentrated, the Germans amassed under Manstein Hausser's Panzer Korps plus five Army Panzer divisions and the *Grossdeutschland* Panzergrenadier Division. In the north, under Kluge, were only six Panzer divisions. These dispositions reflect both the different military attitudes and abilities of Kluge and Manstein, and the different solutions each had arrived at for dealing with the strong Soviet defensive positions. These were formidable. There were six belts of defences, deployed in places to a depth of 110 miles (176 km), consisting of dug-in anti-tank, mortar and machine-gun strongpoints well sited to take on those German armoured units which succeeded in breaking through the intensely dense minefields into the prepared 'killing grounds'. As many as twelve anti-tank guns were deployed in single batteries, although five was the average. The minefields, according to James Dunnigan (*The Russian Front*, Arms and Armour Press, 1978), had a density of 2,400 anti-tank and 2,700 anti-personnel mines per mile of front.

Above left *Leibstandarte tanks and grenadiers in Kharkov* (BA 78/20/0a).

Above *SdKfz 251 outside a field dressing station in Kharkov* (BA 73/100/4).

Below *Goebbels congratulates Sturmbannführer Krass of the Leibstandarte on the award of his Knight's Cross on 5 April 1943. In black Panzer uniform is Max Wünsche* (BPK WII427a).

Leibstandarte Adolf Hitler

Background photograph *Low-flying Ju 87 Stuka returns from a sortie above a quartet of German tanks — a PzKpfw II in the foreground with short-barrelled PzKpfwIVs behind and to the left and a later Mark on the right* (BA 216/403/34a).

Inset *Standartenführer Fritz Witt photographed during the fighting for Kharkov on 31 March 1943. Behind him is Dr Hermann Besuden* (BPK WII232N).

Where the Russians miscalculated was in their assessment of the main assault's direction, which they were convinced would fall in the north. As a result, Rokossovsky faced Kluge in the north with six Armies (each equivalent to a German Korps), giving him a three-to-two superiority in numbers without counting the massive artillery support; while in the south Vatutin's five Armies were effectively outnumbered by six to five. In fact, the odds here were even more in the Germans' favour as they were to concentrate their attack on a very narrow front of less than thirty miles (48 km) which meant that their assault fell on just two of the Russian commander's Armies. However, Marshal Zhukov, 'the Russian Fox', had kept a very strong mobile reserve, the equivalent of four German Korps, and one of these was armoured.

The final line-up gave the German forces 2,700 tanks and assault guns against a Russian total of 3,300; 900,000 infantry versus 1,337,000; 10,000 artillery pieces against no fewer than 20,220 Russian guns; and 2,500 support aircraft, including the tank-busting Henschel Hs 129, against 2,650 Soviet machines (Geoffrey Jukes, *Kursk*, Macdonald, 1969).

The German attack was originally scheduled for 12 June, but the Axis collapse in North Africa and fears of an incipient invasion of southern Europe made Hitler postpone it for three more weeks. Unusually, since most attacks are launched at dawn for mainly psychological reasons, this offensive opened at 15:00 on 4 July—in the south.

Here, Manstein's tactics against the Soviet defences were based upon the 'Panzerkeil' concept —massive armoured wedges headed by the heavy Tiger tanks and the new Elefant self-propelled guns, followed and flanked by the lighter Panthers and PzKpfw IVs, followed in turn by the mechanized infantry units and finally by the slower-moving 'foot-sloggers'. Hausser's Panzer Korps, accompanied by the *Grossdeutschland*, 3rd and 11th Panzer Divisions, opened the attack by moving against the Soviet-controlled higher ground overlooking their positions. This they achieved with some difficulty. . .

Next day, 5 July, Kluge's infantry-heavy forces in the north commenced their own offensive. Here, the tactics employed were different, the infantry going in first to clear the anti-tank gun nests, followed by

31

the Panzers. In this way his 16th Panzer Korps succeeded in dislodging the Russian 15th Rifle Division, but elsewhere progress was extremely slow, and was further hampered by a Soviet artillery bombardment during the night of the 4th/5th which somewhat disrupted German preparations.

On 6 July both German pincers made encouraging headway. In the north, the tanks began exploiting the breach in the dislodged Russian division's positions and reached the high ground north of Kashara. Here, however, it was stalled, and a see-saw armoured battle involving over 1,100 tanks and assault guns on each side developed which was to last four days. In the south, the Army's *Grossdeutschland* Division made the best progress, justifying its élite status by capturing the village of Dubrova and forcing the Russian 3rd Mechanized Corps back to the line of the River Pena, the last obstacle before the important town of Oboyan, which Vatutin had ordered held at all costs.

Paul Hausser's doughty SS Panzer Korps had not been far behind and had made good progress on 6 July, penetrating some twenty miles (32 km) towards Prokhorovka. However, despite the fact that the Russian line was now breached significantly in two places, Kempf's 6th, 7th and 19th Panzer Divisions —which were supposed to provide flank cover for the SS division—had been able to make only slow headway after crossing the River Donets, and were stalled by Shulimov's 7th Guards Army.

At the end of the day the Germans had cause for some measure of optimism, although losses had been high both among the tanks and the infantry, where the Russian artillery superiority had proved its value. On the northern front, briefly, the next few days were a veritable nightmare, though, for Soviet reinforcements seemed to materialize wherever the Panzers moved, and a stalemate was soon reached. In the south a similar situation developed, although here Manstein's tactics produced considerable early successes, particularly for the three SS divisions, the *Grossdeutschland* and the 11th Panzer Division.

On 11 July the battle hung in the balance. Although the German forces were seriously depleted, their immediate Soviet opponents were in even worse shape, the 6th Guards Army which had borne the brunt of the assault being particularly demoralized. However, the Germans were now looking over their shoulders, figuratively speaking,

StuG IIIs and other Leibstandarte vehicles seen from a low-flying aircraft during the Kursk operation (BA 243/2261/33).

as news of the Allied landings in Sicily reached them. Moreover, Hitler was vacillating as usual, not knowing what to do for the best; and the élite Russian 5th Guards Army had arrived in the Kursk salient to bolster the defence after a 225-mile (360-km) march.

The largest single tank battle of the war opened on 12 July between the latter formation and Hausser's SS Korps, as the Soviets finally launched a major counter-attack. Some 850 Russian tanks and self-propelled guns, mostly T-34s and SU-85s, engaged the 700-odd PzKpfw IVs, Tigers and Panthers of Hausser's command. For much of the eight hours that the battle raged the fighting was literally at point-blank range, the lines of tanks interpenetrating and blasting away at each other with every weapon available. At these ranges, superior armour or armament was irrelevant—a 'hit' meant death. Overhead, the Soviet air force battled desperately with the Luftwaffe for command of the skies. Great courage, determination and, indeed, fanaticism was displayed by the tank crews of both sides. The Leibstandarte's hero, and ultimately the greatest tank 'ace' of the war, Michael Wittman, destroyed no fewer than thirty T-34s with his Tiger. However, the end result was inconclusive. It was a Pyrrhic victory for the SS, in that Rotmistrov's forces withdrew first, leaving over 300 burning and blackened tanks on the field; but the Leibstandarte, *Das Reich* and *Totenkopf* had lost a similar number.

Hitler called Manstein and Kluge to a conference in East Prussia. He was obviously very disturbed at the Allied landings in Sicily and wished the battle called off. Manstein was aghast, since he argued that one final effort would clinch things in the Germans' favour. But Hitler was adamant, particularly since the Russians had launched another counter-offensive in the Orel sector, to the north of and therefore behind Kluge's force. For once, Hitler actually wished to withdraw. What is more, he needed the Leibstandarte in Italy. He even, to that individual's disgust, needed 'Sepp' Dietrich in person to escort Mussolini's mistress, Clara Pettachi, to her lover after the Italian dictator had been deposed and then valiantly rescued from Gran Sasso by Otto Skorzeny! Nor were the men of the division itself pleased at the transfer from where they felt they belonged. In north Italy they were not helping to throw back the Anglo-American invaders, but were acting just as a private

Left and below left *The bleak conditions under which the Leibstandarte had to try to fight its way out of the Kamenets-Podolsk pocket are clearly shown in these two photographs of rather the worse for wear PzKpfw IVs (BA 578/1945/23 & 708/298/21).*

Right *Michael Wittman and crew, including Balthasar Wohl, his gunner, during a phase in the hectic Normandy campaign. This and the following photo were probably taken to commemorate Wittman's award of the Swords to accompany the Oakleaves to his Knight's Cross (BA 299/1802/2).*

Hitler's Teutonic Knights

army for Mussolini. For want of another foe, they were used in anti-partisan duties. The little town of Boves suffered accordingly—the Leibstandarte massacred virtually every man, woman and child apart from a pitiful handful of accidental survivors. The Leibstandarte, and the local Italians, were probably equally grateful, though for different reasons, when the division was recalled to Russia in November.

During the Leibstandarte's absence from Russia, all hell had broken loose. The Orel offensive swept all before it and by the end of August Kharkov had been recaptured by the Soviet Army yet again, followed by Melitopol and Kiev. The Leibstandarte engaged the enemy with refreshed determination, smashing a heavy concentration of T-34s at Shev-shentka. Shortly afterwards, when *Wiking* and *Wallonien* had desperately fought their way out of the Cherkassy pocket, the Leibstandarte, together with 1st and 16th Panzer Divisions, was itself trapped alongside some 2,500 men of *Das Reich* in a new Soviet encirclement at Kamenets-Podolsk. Lacking the strength to break out, it had to be rescued by two of the new SS Panzer Divisions, *Hohenstaufen* and *Frundsberg*.

The Leibstandarte was again recalled to France to rest and be brought back up to strength, and its next operations were going to be against a new but equally determined enemy. When the Allies poured ashore in Normandy on 6 June 1944, the Leibstandarte was encamped at Bruges, in Belgium. On D-Day plus one the division was ordered to move towards Caen. Movement by day was rendered perilous by the swarms of rocket-firing Allied fighter-bombers which roamed the skies. Gone for the Panzers were the halcyon days of the headlong advance while Stukas screamed overhead. Now the battle became a desperate struggle for every ditch and coppice in the dense Normandy bocage. With the fighting at such close quarters, the SS Tigers lost their normal advantage of heavy armour and armament, and the lighter Allied Shermans—particularly the British Sherman Firefly—were able to engage them on more equal terms. Nevertheless, the Leibstandarte achieved some notable victories, few more so than the engagement in July when Montgomery launched Operation 'Goodwood' in an attempt to break out of the Caen sector.

A column of Cromwell tanks of the 7th Armoured

Division (the famous 'Desert Rats') was advancing along a narrow, high-hedged road overlooked by a low wooded hill. Here, hidden, were five Tigers commanded by the Leibstandarte's tank 'ace', Michael Wittman, whose personal 'score' now exceeded 120. Waiting until the Cromwells were well along the lane, Wittman's tanks opened fire, first knocking out the leading and last vehicles in the column. The remaining 58 Cromwells milled about, unable to move forwards or back and unable to climb the steep banks of the lane. In a matter of minutes Wittman's five Tigers had eliminated 25 of the Cromwells. By this time, however, the burning tank which had blocked the British soldiers' retreat had been dragged clear and they were able to get away. (Wittman himself was killed shortly afterwards when his own Tiger was surrounded by five Allied Shermans. His body lay in an unmarked grave until 1983 when it was reinterred with proper military honours in the cemetery at La Cambe.)

At the end of July the Americans finally succeeded

in breaking out from the beach-head at Avranches and started spilling out into Brittany. The Leibstandarte, together with *Das Reich*, the 2nd and 116th Panzer Divisions and the 17th SS Panzergrenadier Division *Götz von Berlichingen*, under the overall command of Paul Hausser, were assembled to stem the advance. The plan was that they would advance from Mortain through Avranches into the gap left between General Patton's advancing Third Army and the balance of the Allied troops still trapped in the beach-head. It was a forlorn hope. The SS divisions were massacred by Allied fighter-bombers, particularly the rocket-firing Typhoons of the RAF's 245 Squadron, whose operations during the battle of Mortain are so graphically described in John Golley's fine book *The Day of the Typhoon* (Patrick Stephens, 1986). Stubbornly, the survivors tried to keep up the attack even when Hausser knew in his heart that the task was impossible. When they did finally acknowledge defeat and tried to retire, it was almost too late. The bulk of the divisions were trapped by an Allied encirclement in the Falaise-Argentan area, ever afterwards known as the Falaise Pocket, and only strenuous efforts by the *Hitlerjugend* Division kept open a narrow avenue through which the bulk of the

Left *One of the most famous pictures of the war, this shows Michael Wittman shortly before his death, and is well posed to show off his full regalia* (BA 299/1802/8).

Right *Tiger of the 2nd Company, 1st SS Panzer Korps* (BA 299/1805/20).

SS survivors could escape. Nevertheless, the Germans left 10,000 dead in the pocket and the Allies took 50,000 prisoners.

The Leibstandarte and other survivors now began the long retreat across France, and the SS divisions were shortly withdrawn to Germany as a lull emerged in the fighting. The Allies had over-extended themselves and needed time to regroup and to allow supplies to catch up with the leading formations. Many tanks were literally out of both fuel and ammunition. So, Hitler began planning his 'last throw', in which the Leibstandarte would play a significant role.

Hitler's scheme was flawless in principle. The only way the Germans could regain the initiative was by a massive counter-offensive. The strategy and the planned direction of the assault—through the Ardennes, as in 1940—could not have been bettered. But it was a forlorn gamble because, even though the SS divisions were reinforced to such a degree that they were stronger than at any previous time during the war, Germany as a whole lacked the strength to sustain another major blitzkrieg.

The plan was to cut a swathe in between the US First and Third Armies and head for Antwerp, which would deprive the Allies of their main port of supply. Then, it was reasoned, the German divisions could roll up the British and Canadian armies which had been thwarted at Arnhem. The plan envisaged a strong thrust by three Armies: in the north would be 'Sepp' Dietrich's 6th Panzer Army; Dietrich himself had been promoted in August 1944 and the Leibstandarte was now commanded by Wilhelm Mohnke. Its objective was to sweep through Malmédy, bypass Liège and head straight for Antwerp. In the centre would be Hasso von Manteuffel's 5th Panzer Army which would head for the River Meuse at Namur and then on to Brussels. Protecting the southern flank of the attack would be 7th

Right *Wittman's Tiger after having been disabled during the fighting for Villers-Bocage. All the crew escaped this encounter* (BA 494/3376/10a).

Inset *Often described as the remains of Wittman's Tiger, this is in fact a destroyed vehicle of schwere SS Panzer Abteilung 102 outside Evrecy in mid-July 1944* (BA 494/3397/4a).

More of the destruction in Villers Bocage (BA 494/3376/8a, 9a, 13a & 14a).

Army, led by Erich Brandenberger, which would advance through Bastogne, south of Dinant and on to the River Sambre.

The 6th Panzer Army comprised the Leibstandarte together with *Das Reich, Hohenstaufen* and *Hitlerjugend* bolstered by the 3rd Fallschirmjäger Division and four Volksgrenadier divisions. Hitler placed great faith in 'Sepp' Dietrich but, alas, Operation *Wacht am Rhein* was not to prove a success for the SS and, to their chagrin, both Manteuffel's Panzers and the second-rate 7th Army would progress further. In fact, the only unit to make any real headway was the Leibstandarte Kampfgruppe of some 5,000 men commanded by the dashing but totally ruthless Joachim Peiper.

At 05:30 on the morning of 16 December 1944, preceded by an intensive artillery barrage which rocked the unprepared and unsuspecting men of the two American divisions in the path of the German assault, Peiper's battlegroup spearheaded the Leibstandarte's advance, heading for Stavelot and the Amblève valley. To begin with movement was slow because of the appalling road conditions, and it was not long before Peiper's tanks began to run low on fuel. Then the battlegroup's reconnaissance battalion discovered an American fuel dump at Büllingen. Some fifty American soldiers were taken prisoner and forced to refuel the thirsty tanks. Worse

was to follow. Peiper had divided his battlegroup into two columns, each taking a different route towards Ligneuville. The second column overtook and surprised a small group of stragglers from the American 7th Armoured Division who were heading towards St Vith. The only American officer to survive what followed, 1st Lieutenant Virgil T. Lary, gave the following testimony at Nuremberg.

'It was decided that it would be best to surrender to this overwhelming force, the First *Adolf Hitler* SS Panzer Division, as we learned later. This we did. . . We were all placed in this field, approximately 150 to 160, maybe 175 men. . . The Germans then, at the particular time, were continuing to advance in a southerly direction towards Bastogne, and one of their self-propelled 88 mm guns was ordered to stop, and it was backed around facing the group of personnel as they were standing in the field. After what happened, I have no doubt today that if they had been able to depress the muzzle of this gun into our group, they would have fired at point-blank range with their artillery into that group of men. They were not able to do that, however, because we were more or less in a depression below the gun and they couldn't lower it. So this particular self-propelled weapon was blocking their advance and it was ordered off. At that time they drove up two half-tracks and parked them facing the group, at a fifteen

or twenty foot interval between the two. A man stood up in this vehicle, who I later identified at Dachau, and fired a pistol. . .into the group. At the time we ordered our men to stand fast because we knew if they made a break that they would have a right then to cut loose on us with their machine-guns.

'His first shot killed my driver. The second shot that he fired into the group then set off a group of machine-guns firing into this helpless group of unarmed American prisoners-of-war. Those of us who were not killed immediately in the initial burst fell to the ground. . . We continued to lay on the ground and the fire continued to come into us. . . When they ceased firing after approximately five minutes, maybe three minutes, they came into the group to those men who were still alive, and of course writhing in agony, and they shot them in the head. . . During the initial firing I was only hit one time.'

Later, as dusk fell, Virgil Lary dragged himself across a fence and hid under a pile of logs in a wood-shed. The next day, he succeeded in reaching the

Above *'Sepp' Dietrich with other Army and SS officers during an inspection of the Leibstandarte in 1944* (BPK WII107).

Right *Tigers of the 1st and 2nd Companies of the 1st SS Panzer Korps in 1944* (BA 738/267/18 & 299/1805/16).

American lines where his story was received with incredulity.

There are discrepancies in this account because, when the advancing Americans following up the German retreat later discovered the bodies lying in the field, there were 71 of them. Twenty men had survived. This is far fewer than 175 or even 150, and lends credence to the testimony of the man responsible for the massacre, Oberschütze Georg Fleps, that he had opened fire when some of the Americans had run for the woods. It was still an appalling deed.

At Nuremberg, Joachim Peiper—who, as commander of the battlegroup, took ultimate responsibility for the massacre—was sentenced to death by hanging. He asked if he could be shot by military

firing squad instead, and his request was granted. After five years in Landsberg prison, however, his sentence was commuted, as were those passed on many other Waffen-SS officers convicted of war crimes. He eventually settled in Traves, in south-eastern France. In 1975, his face was recognized by a shopkeeper in nearby Vesoul. The shopkeeper, whose name was Cacheu, was a member of the French communist party and had fought in the Resistance during the war. The news of his discovery eventually reached a French journalist, Pierre Durand. After extensive investigation, Durand assured himself that the man in the house overlooking the River Saône at Traves was the wartime Waffen-SS officer, and he published his findings in *L'Humanité*. Peiper began to receive threats, and harassment from some of his neighbours. He was warned to leave France by 14 July, Bastille Day.

Peiper, armed with a pistol and a rifle, refused to leave, although he sent his wife and teenage daughter away. On the evening of 14 July he took these weapons with him to sit on the balcony of his house, his two guard dogs alongside him. During the night, the sound of shots was heard. When the Gendarmerie arrived, Peiper was a charred corpse in a blazing house. But it was obvious that his fighting spirit had been undiminished thirty years after the war: one cartridge had been fired from his rifle and only one shell was left in his pistol. His murderers have never been caught.

Returning to the Ardennes in that bleak midwinter: Peiper's troops reached Ligneuville and helped themselves to the still-hot food which had been left by the Americans in their hasty retreat. Then it was onward towards Stavelot. Two Sherman tanks which blocked the route were soon disposed of, but then the Leibstandarte battlegroup reached the high ground overlooking the river— and saw what appeared to be a massive concentration of American forces on the other side. As it happened, it was a comparatively small unit of engineers hastily trying to complete a road block. But they administered a psychological check and Peiper, exhausted, decided to sleep on the problem—while sending out reconnaissance units to seek other possible avenues. In the morning, refreshed, his Leibstandarte battlegroup charged forward full of confidence. They stormed the narrow stone bridge and Stavelot was theirs. At Trois Ponts, the next village, they received another

check. There, the American defenders had but one 57 mm anti-tank gun. The surprise of its fire was, however, enough to give their engineers time to destroy the bridges across the river. The anti-tank gun's crew was wiped out—but Peiper had to find another avenue of advance.

He headed for La Gleize, but en route a brief break in the heavy snow-cloud cover which had assisted the German advance enabled American P-47 Thunderbolt fighter-bombers to roar into the attack. For two hours the deadly assault continued. When Peiper reached the next bridge, it, too, had been destroyed. He ordered a retreat on La Gleize, then changed his route towards Stoumont. By the time his tanks reached this objective, Stavemont had been recaptured by the Americans in his rear. There, another atrocity by men of Peiper's battlegroup was discovered: 26 civilians suspected of having harboured American troops had been slaughtered out of hand. At Stoumont, fighting was fierce, particularly around the sanatorium of St Edward. The SS eventually triumphed, but it was a hollow victory: the retreat to La Gleize went ahead as planned.

The Americans were now fighting with the same fanatical determination as the SS, and a 'no prisoners' order had gone out following dissemination of the news about the Malmédy massacre. What had happened to the rest of 6th SS Panzer Army? To a large extent, it had been halted by the weather and the terrain, which were far different in the Ardennes in December from what they had been in May four years previously. Roads were impassable for the tanks, whose tracks slithered and slid into ravines and ditches on the ice and snow. A huge traffic jam developed. Hausser had veritably 'come unstuck' and had to swallow SS pride in order to detach *Das Reich* to join Manteuffel's 5th Panzer Army, which *was* making headway. Peiper was forced to withdraw from La Gleize, leaving forty per cent of his men and equipment destroyed or captured behind him.

On 8 January 1945 Hitler at last realized the hopelessness of the situation in the Ardennes, where the assault had finally and irrevocably been halted by the rapid redeployment of George Patton's Third Army, and he recalled 6th SS Panzer Army. Again the SS divisions were refitted. Now the 6th Army was to be committed to Hungary, where *Wiking* and *Totenkopf* had failed. They were to lift the siege of Budapest, relieve the gar-

Above left *Camouflaged jacket being worn by a Leibstandarte Unterscharführer* (BA 469/3471/17).

Above right *SS Panzer jacket with camouflage cap being worn by an Unterscharführer* (BA 297/1725/33).

rison there, and throw the Russians back.

Hampered by the weather and the severely disrupted rail transport, the depleted and demoralized SS divisions arrived in Hungary at the beginning of March. Making good progress against the Russian hordes to begin with, by the middle of the month they were finally at the end of their tether and began to retreat. Hitler, in a towering rage, feeling that even his beloved Leibstandarte had turned traitor, ordered the divisions to strip off their armbands. Dietrich is sometimes said to have sent all his own medals and decorations back to Hitler in reply, although this may be apocryphal. 'That's all the thanks we get', he is reported to have said.

Grudgingly, like the other SS divisions, the Leibstandarte retreated into Austria. After Hitler's suicide, the division surrendered to the Americans at Steyr, although some of its rearguard was captured by the Russians. The Führer Begleit Bataillon, Hitler's personal guard selected from members of the division, died in Berlin defending its Führer's ashes.

2. 2nd SS Panzer Division
Das Reich

By the time that SS Division *Das Reich* was withdrawn from the front line in Russia in March 1942 for rest and refit as a Panzer division, it had already taken part in four campaigns and had suffered over 20,000 casualties in Russia alone.

The division's origins dated back to October 1933 when the SS Standarte *Deutschland* had been formed from a Bavarian Allgemeine-SS police unit under the command of Majors Sagerer and Lieber. A second Standarte, *Germania*, was formed in August of the following year, in Hamburg, by Hauptsturmführer Wilhelm Bittrich (the later victor at Arnhem, and one of the most courageous, talented and chivalrous of all Waffen-SS commanders). A third Standarte, *Der Führer*, was formed in Vienna in March 1938. *Deutschland* and *Germania* were originally of battalion size, but in 1936, after service in the SS-VT (VT = Verfügungstruppe) became regarded as military service with the armed forces, they were each expanded to the size of regiments, with three battalions apiece.

In October 1936 the SS-VT also acquired its own general staff, in the form of the SS-VT Inspectorate under the overall command of Paul Hausser. Born in 1880, Hausser had been in the regular Army for 33 years prior to joining the SS; he commanded the SS-VT Division (later renamed *Das Reich*) from October 1939 until the same month in 1941 before being promoted to Korps commander as the Waffen-SS

Left A Reich *StuG III sporting the* Deutschland *Regiment's device during the invasion of Russia in 1941* (BA 596/395/29).

expanded. (Hausser lived in Ludwigsburg and died in 1972.)

Although the SS-VT Division was not formally constituted until October 1939, elements of the three Standarten took part in the invasion of Poland, under Wehrmacht command. *Deutschland*, together with the SS artillery regiment and motor cycle, reconnaissance and signals battalions, fought in Kampfgruppe 'Kempf', named after its commander, Generalleutnant Kempf. *Germania* was seconded to 14th Army on the right flank of the attack, where it took part in the occupation of the industrial zone of Poland and advanced into the Lemberg area. The remainder of the SS-VT units participated in 3rd Army's advance through Mlawa and Praschnitz, crossing the rivers Narew and Bug, and capped their first victorious campaign by taking the Polish fortress of Modlin by storm.

After the Polish campaign the participating units were sent back to Neidenburg, East Prussia, to be re-formed as a true SS division. Each of the three intrinsic regiments—*Deutschland*, *Germania* and *Der Führer*—at this time comprised three battalions, each of three companies. Each company had nine machine-guns, two anti-tank guns and three mortars. In addition, each battalion had an attached heavy weapons company with six heavy mortars and eight anti-tank guns; and each regiment incorporated a motorized anti-tank company with twelve guns; a towed artillery company with between six and eight 7.5 cm guns; and a motor cycle recce company. The SS-VT Division (mot), as it was now known, also included an anti-tank battalion of three companies; a motor cycle recce battalion of two companies; an artillery regiment of three battalions, each of three companies with four guns to a company; signals and pioneer truppen; and a machine-gun battalion, plus supporting troops (supply, medical, etc). Renamed, for no particularly good reason, SS-Verfügungsdivision in April 1940, it was with this force that the formation went to war in the fateful summer of that year.

The *Der Führer* Regiment came under the command of 10th Korps HQ and stormed the strongly defended Grebbe Line in Holland, pushing through to Amsterdam, while the main body of the division followed up 9th Panzer Division and first went into action against the French and Dutch west of Rysbergen. The *Deutschland* Regiment especially distinguished itself in the heavy fighting for Flushing, through the flooded polders and minefields, but only succeeded in capturing the 1¼-mile (2-km) causeway to the island of Walcheren after Luftwaffe aid had been summoned.

Withdrawn from Holland on 18 May, the division was marched by night through Belgium to Flanders where it took part in the battle of Arras, as part of von Kleist's Panzergruppe. It was then turned north to take over protection of the German right flank against Allied forces which were trying to break out of Belgium to the west, and had a particularly hard battle against British troops in Nieppe Wood from 27 to 29 May, since the British had tanks and the SS at this time did not.

After disengaging from this successful action, the division was allowed a brief rest before being marched south to link up with von Reichenau's 6th Army, subsequently going in with the second wave of the attack on the Weygand Line on 5 June. After crossing the River Somme, the SS troops broke through to the rear of the French positions and were soon on the road through Soissons to Troyes. Their last heavy battle of the campaign occurred on 16 June against French troops trying to escape west from the Maginot Line; they then took part in the victorious pursuit, marching via Orleans and Bordeaux south to the Spanish frontier by 27 June. After a brief period spent guarding the border with Vichy France and the occupied part of the Biscay coastline, the division was marched back to Holland, finishing the year near Vesoul.

At the beginning of December 1940 the SS-Regiment *Germania* was transferred from the SS-V Division to join other SS units, mostly of 'ethnic' Germanic origin from occupied countries (see Chapter 4), in the creation of a new division, originally named *Germania* but later rechristened *Wiking*. On 3 December the SS-V Division, strengthened by a battalion from the *Totenkopf* Division (see Chapter 3), was renamed SS-Division *Deutschland*; however, it was thought that this might cause confusion with the Army's *Grossdeutschland* formation, and at the end of January 1941 the division was again renamed, this time as SS-Division *Reich*.

After Mussolini misguidedly decided that it was time Italy played some part in the war and invaded Greece, a coup d'état put Yugoslavia in the Allied camp and German units, including the SS divisions Leibstandarte *Adolf Hitler* and *Reich* as well as the Army's *Grossdeutschland*, became involved in a hurried and makeshift face-saving exercise to bolster the wretched Italian cause. *Reich* was force-marched via Vienna to Romania, where it fell under General Reinhardt's command again. Paul Hausser, in *Waffen-SS im Einsatz*, describes the operations:

'The operation against Belgrade, the capital city, started with the main troop concentrations south of the Rivers Drau and Danube. Only Reinhardt's Panzer Korps was employed north of the rivers for mopping up the Banat and Batschka provinces. It seemed hopeless to try and reach Belgrade from north of the Danube. Nevertheless, an assault party under [Hauptsturmführer] Klingenberg of the motor cycle battalion got hold of a motor boat and, after a hazardous journey, managed to enter Belgrade and force the Mayor to hand over the city. Reconnaissance troops of the Army Group, south of the Danube, reached this strongpoint probably at the same time, if not earlier. However, the city was handed over to Klingenberg' (who later became a divisional commander and was killed in 1945).

After a short rest south-west of Linz, in Austria, the division was transferred to Poland, where it was

Right *In jovial mood, Himmler and other SS officers with a Russian youth. On Himmler's right are Karl Wolff and Hauptsturmführer Josef Kiermeir* (BPK WII163 F 3842a)

Fighting on the Terek front in September 1942 (BPK WII152 3276a).

PzKpfw III on the move through grass which has been set alight by artillery fire (BPK WII153 F 4374).

Above and below *Men of the SS-VT during the invasion of France in June 1940* (BA 75/118/32 & 33).

Left *PzKpfw III moves past a 3.7 cm Pak 35/36* (BPK WII153 F 3277a).

to take part in the momentous invasion of Russia as part of Guderian's 2nd Panzergruppe in Von Bock's Army Group Centre.

At 3:30 on the morning of 22 June 1941 the German frontier with Russia disappeared under a dense pall of smoke as an intense artillery barrage opened up. Then the tanks and half-tracks rolled forward, and Operation 'Barbarossa' was under way. The SS-Division *Reich* was grouped with the 10th Panzer Division and elements of the *Grossdeutschland* Regiment in the 46th Panzer Korps, under the command of General Freiherr von Vietinghoff. This Korps formed the 2nd Panzergruppe reserve and acted in support of the other divisions forcing a crossing over the River Bug either side of the ancient fortress of Brest-Litovsk. For these operations the *Reich* Division had been strengthened by the addition of a battalion of StuG (Sturmgeschutz) III assault guns.

The 46th Panzer Korps did not get into action properly until 26 June, when it was brought up to safeguard the left flank of the Panzergruppe against mounting Soviet resistance, and then it participated in the highly successful encirclement of large numbers of Russian troops in the Bialystock pocket. By 2 July the Korps had reached the River Beresina, where elements of the motor cycle reconnaissance battalion *Reich* managed after hard fighting to secure a bridgehead ten miles south of Beresino. Despite conflicting orders from the High Command, Heinz Guderian decided that it was vital to maintain the momentum of his Gruppe's advance towards its first major objective, Smolensk, and he ordered a general push towards the line of the River Dnieper. During this operation *Reich* again provided flank guard, this time on the right, in the vicinity of Pavlovo. The Dnieper was crossed with remarkably light casualties, and 46th Panzer Korps, including the SS-Division *Reich*, was now ordered to advance via Gorki-Pochinok to Yelnya, while guarding its right flank against a Soviet troop concentration around Mogilev. This task was entrusted to the *Grossdeutschland* Regiment, while the 10th Panzer Division and *Reich*, accompanied personally by Guderian himself, pushed on towards Gorki, which they reached on 14 July after heavy fighting and severe casualties, particularly among the artillery. On the 15th, advance elements of 2nd Panzergruppe (29th Motorized Infantry Division) reached the out-

Background photograph *StuG IIIF with long-barrelled 7.5 cm gun in winter camouflage* (BA 84/3416/18a).

Inset *Tiger Is and grenadiers of an unidentified SS unit* (BA 277/846/10).

54

Three of the leading figures in Das Reich. **Far left and far right** *Paul Hausser*. **Centre left and right** *Werner Ostendorrf*. **Left and below right** *Fritz Klingenberg* (Left, Christopher Ailsby Historical Archives; right, BA 77/93/34, 74/44/64 & 77/93/33).

skirts of Smolensk, while 10th Panzer and *Reich* spearheaded a drive south of the city and reached Yelnya in the face of determined Russian counterattacks from fortified positions. Here, they held on for several days despite running very low on ammunition, and on 22 July took 1,100 prisoners and knocked out fifty Russian tanks.

Guderian 'visited the foremost unit, the motor cyclists under command of the brave Hauptsturmführer Klingenberg, as I wished to gain a personal impression of the terrain and the situation'. This visit convinced him that the planned attack towards Dorogobush in the north, designed to link up with Hoth's 3rd Panzergruppe, would have to be delayed. Soviet pressure was mounting all the time and, on 27 July, the badly mauled 10th Panzer Division was withdrawn from the line for a rest, its place alongside *Reich* being taken by the 268th Infantry Division.

At this point in the advance, despite the fact that General Hoth had succeeded in trapping no fewer than ten Russian divisions in the Smolensk pocket, Hitler made the fateful decision to call off an immediate thrust towards Moscow, and directed

Guderian's 2nd Panzergruppe to disengage and march south-west towards Gomel to collaborate with the 2nd Army in another large encirclement. Dedicating himself to the task with determination if not with enthusiasm, Guderian asked for and received reinforcements and began planning the initial stages of the operation, which necessitated the capture of the important communications centre of Roslavl. SS *Reich* was not involved in this operation, being entrusted instead with the defence of the left flank of the Yelnya salient. Roslavl fell on 1 August after a single day's struggle and four Russian divisions were surrounded, but *Reich* was still involved in heavy defensive fighting, being faced by some eleven divisions, two of them armoured! On 8 August *Reich* was withdrawn for a badly needed rest and refit north-east of Smolensk, and did not therefore take part in the initial stages of the southern push. This proceeded well to begin with but was running into difficulties by the end of the month, and on 2 September *Reich* was ordered back into the fray.

Guderian again visited the division near Avdeivka

Above *Reich StuG III in summer 1941* (BA 77/93/32).

Below *PzKpfw IV of the same unit* (BA 77/93/15).

Hitler's Teutonic Knights

Above *Reich SdKfz 221 light armoured car* (BA 77/93/24).

Below Reich *infantry and armoured cars cross a Russian bridge* (Christopher Ailsby Historical Archives).

on the 3rd, where he met Hausser and 'told him to be prepared to attack Sosnitza on the 4th'. Unfortunately, that evening it began to rain, the dusty roads turned to mud and two-thirds of SS-Division *Reich* became completely bogged down and unable to advance. Determination prevailed, however, and the division succeeded in capturing its objective on the 5th.

Guderian 'spent 6 December again with SS-*Das Reich* (sic). It was engaged in attacking the railway bridge over the Desna, near Makoshino. I went to some trouble to provide air support for this. As a result of the bad roads the whole division was not assembled. On the way there I passed a number of its units, some on the march, others resting in the woods. The excellent discipline of the troops made a first-class impression and they loudly expressed their satisfaction at once more forming part of the Panzergruppe.'

During the ensuing engagement the division was assigned to the right flank of Guderian's forces, now renamed Panzerarmee *Guderian*, providing the point of contact with the 2nd Army. Bad roads continued to make progress extremely difficult, and aerial reconnaissance was impossible, but the Kiev pocket was finally sealed, trapping the better part of five Soviet Armies.

SS-Division *Reich* was at this time transferred to the eastern wing of the German salient, and captured the town of Romny. On 18 September a crisis developed as the Russians threw in two fresh divisions, one of them armoured, against the town, supported by heavy bombing raids from the air. Nevertheless, *Reich* held firm and five days later was spearheading yet another offensive, in conjunction with the 4th Panzer Division, east of Kamlicha. On 26 September the hard-fought battle of Kiev came to a close with the surrender of some 665,000 Russian soldiers and a vast collection of tanks and guns. It was a worthwhile victory, but two months had elapsed, the good weather had almost passed, the troops were more tired than elated, and Moscow was to prove an impossible prize.

General Günther Blumentritt, Chief of Staff of the 4th Army during Operation 'Barbarossa' and later commander of the 12th SS Korps, has written

that 'the great encirclement battles had led to the capture of huge numbers of prisoners and vast quantities of booty. But the results were not quite as satisfactory as they might appear at first glance. For one thing those great encirclements made very heavy demands on our Panzer forces. For another, they were never entirely successful and large groups of the enemy frequently slipped out of the pockets eastwards.' *

Later, General Blumentritt recalls, 'when Moscow itself was almost in sight, the mood both of commanders and troops changed. With amazement and disappointment we discovered in late October and early November that the beaten Russians seemed quite unaware that as a military force they had almost ceased to exist.'

Operation 'Taifun', the attack on Moscow, opened on 30 September in brilliant autumnal sunshine with Guderian's forces beginning their advance through Gluchov towards Orel. SS-Division *Reich* formed part of the spearhead again, together with three Panzer divisions, a motorized division and the *Grossdeutschland* Regiment. On 6 October the division was entrusted with the task of cutting the Smolensk-Moscow road between Gzhatsk and Vyasma, completing an encirclement around the latter town. Despite fierce opposition, including continuous strafing by Soviet fighters which Göring had boasted were 'non-existent', this phase of the operation was completed satisfactorily with the capture of the road and rail bridges at Yegorye Kuleshi on the first evening, Kamyonka on the second and Nikolskoya on the third, leaving the division firmly astride the main highway to Moscow. Unfortunately, by this time the weather had broken and when the division moved off at dawn on 9 October it was into the teeth of a howling blizzard.

A three-battalion attack by the division's *Deutschland* Regiment succeeded in capturing Gzhatsk and 500 prisoners, while *Der Führer* pressed on along the highway and took two further villages; the division's motor cycle battalion also wiped out a Soviet transport column. Strong Russian reinforcements held up *Reich*'s advance for the next two days, though, *Der Führer* in particular suffering heavy casualties. On 11 October, SS-Division *Reich* was

Left *The rigours of the Russian winter made mobile operations difficult* (BA 213/264/14).

The Fateful Decisions, edited by William Richardson and Seymour Freidin (Consul Books, 1965).

Three faces of war. **Above**—*victory:* Reich *troops with a captured Soviet flag.* **Above right**—*fear: a* Reich *grenadier in the assault.* **Below right**—*cold: men of the* Der Führer *Regiment during the advance on Moscow* (BA 77/93/16, 73/83/58 & 75/119/14).

once more committed to the offensive, with Mozhaisk as its major objective. The Red Army troops, supported by tanks and artillery from an armoured train, fought with fanatical determination to rival that of the Waffen-SS, launching attack after attack, but they still failed to close the breaches driven through their lines. The assault was renewed on the 12th and the village of Shulevo was captured, by which time the Russians were in full retreat along the whole line. Kalinin fell on the 14th, but then reinforcements were rushed to the Mozhaisk sector and hung on doggedly.

The historic battleground of Borodino, site of one of the bloodiest head-on encounters of the Napoleonic Wars, fell to a single German regiment on the 15th: *Der Führer*. The SS-Division *Reich* was then entrusted with the capture of the important crossroads four miles (6 km) to the south-west of Mozhaisk. The cornerstone village of Artemki fell on the 17th, but the closer the SS troops approached the

crossroads, the fiercer the opposition grew and the division's lack of tanks became critical as its StuG IIIs were no match for the Soviet T-34 tanks. Nevertheless, the crossroads was reached on the 18th and by 15:00 two battalions of the *Deutschland* Regiment had entered Mozhaisk itself, supported by tanks from the 10th Panzer Division. Here the Russians fought even more ferociously, and for a time it seemed as though the SS troops would be ejected. Then Klingenberg's motor cycle detachment found a weak spot in the enemy line which Hausser immediately exploited, driving on down the Moscow highway towards Mikhailovskaya.

On the 21st a surprise attack on its flank by fresh Mongolian troops halted the *Deutschland* Regiment, but, despite temperatures of fifteen degrees below freezing and inadequate winter clothing, the Waffen-SS fought back; they took Mikhailovskaya, then Grachevo and Pushkino, but were halted by enfilading fire in front of Borosivo. After artillery

support had been rushed up, though, this town also fell, on 22 October.

Moscow was only forty miles (64 km) away, but SS-Division *Reich* had 'shot its bolt' for the time being. In three weeks it had lost nearly 7,000 killed, wounded and missing; and although frost hardened the road surfaces and improved the going—allowing the Germans to get within eighteen miles (29 km) of Moscow in one place—by the end of November it had become obvious that the city was not going to fall that winter. The Soviet Marshal Zhukov's defences were too strong, and the majority of German units were too tired, depleted and cold to go on any longer. General Blumentritt describes the situation:

'Only for a few hours each day was there limited visibility at the front. Until 09:00 the wintry landscape was shrouded in a thick fog. Gradually, a red ball, the sun, became visible in the eastern sky and by about 11:00 it was possible to see a little. At 15:00 dusk set in, and an hour later it was almost completely dark again.

'Supplies were short. Yet in order to encourage the soldiers. . . trainloads of red wine were shipped to us from France and Germany. The anger of a unit which received a trainload of wine instead of the shells it urgently needed can be readily imagined.

'There could be no question of digging in; the ground was frozen to the consistency of iron.

'At night it was often necessary to keep small fires burning underneath our tanks, lest the engines freeze and burst.'

Under these circumstances, it is little wonder that Marshal Zhukov's counter-offensive, launched at the beginning of December with no fewer than eighteen divisions, succeeded in recapturing almost all of the principal objectives seized during Operation 'Taifun'.

SS-Division *Reich* suffered heavily in the winter defensive fighting before Moscow—a further 4,000 casualties by mid-February—and in March 1942 it was withdrawn from the line and sent to north-west France to recuperate, have its strength brought up to scratch, and be re-formed as a Panzergrenadier division. By the time the reconstituted division returned to the Russian Front at the beginning of 1943 it would in fact be a fully fledged Panzer division.

Two mixed battalions from the decimated *Deutschland* and *Der Führer* Regiments did remain in Russia during this period, as a battlegroup under the command of Werner Ostendorff, who would later command the whole division for a brief while. Back in France, the transfused division, now finally re-christened *Das Reich*, fell under the command of Gruppenführer Georg Keppler. Apart from the re-inforced parent units, the division included the new SS-Kradschützen (motor cycle) Regiment *Langemarck*, which took part in the vain German attempt to prevent the scuttling of the French Fleet at Toulon in November. Apart from this, the division saw no action during the remainder of 1942, but was thrust back into the rigours of the Russian campaign,

Hitler's Teutonic Knights

together with the Leibstandarte *Adolf Hitler* and the *Totenkopf* Divisions, in January 1943: the year of crisis for Germany.

The sweeping German advances of 1942 had over-extended their lines, von Paulus' 6th Army had finally surrendered at Stalingrad, the Americans had come into the war following the Japanese attack on Pearl Harbor, Rommel had been defeated at the second battle of Alamein, and it seemed that German forces were in retreat on all fronts. However, no-one had reckoned with Paul Hausser's new SS Panzer Korps, his three divisions of hardened veterans which were now attached to Army Group South (Don). A finger of fire and steel was about to be inserted into the dike.

After advancing into Kharkov during February, the new SS Panzer Korps was temporarily threatened by encirclement from strong Soviet forces and, despite a hysterical 'hold at all costs' order from Hitler, Hausser took the courageous decision to evacuate and withdraw his divisions behind the River Uda. SS *Das Reich* made a sixty-mile (96-km) march on the 16th to close a gap in the German lines, essential to General von Manstein's plan of drawing the Russian forces into a trap. By 9 March Hausser was in a position to launch an attack to recapture Kharkov, which he did on the 10th. *Das Reich* and the Leibstandarte *Adolf Hitler* formed the spearhead of this operation, bringing into action for the first time their new complement of PzKpfw VI Tiger I tanks. As a result, the city fell in only five days, albeit after

cruelly bitter fighting.

Both sides again paused to regroup and rethink. Both were exhausted—an infantryman would probably have used a stronger term. However, von Manstein had succeeded in stabilizing the German line with the exception of a large Russian salient to the north of Kharkov, around Kursk, and the German position was unquestionably stronger than it had been a mere month earlier. Moreover, although the disaster at Stalingrad and the long retreat from the Caucasus Mountains, which had been reached at such expense in 1942, were tragic from the German point of view, lines of communication and supply had been shortened and the Wehrmacht now enjoyed a higher density of troops in the front line than at any previous time during the Russian campaign. Whether future German operations were to be strategically offensive or defensive, however, the Kursk salient had to be eliminated.

Unfortunately for the Waffen-SS, the attack was delayed too long, for a variety of reasons, allowing the Russians time to build up their defences in the salient—to lay extensive minefields, to establish anti-tank 'killing grounds' and to lay in strong mobile reserves. In the event, Operation 'Zitadelle' did not get off the ground until 4 July. In the southern sector the SS Panzer Korps formed the spearhead of 4th Panzer Army, the 'right hook' of a pincer movement designed to entrap the Soviet forces concentrated around Kursk. Von Mellenthin observed that the terrain 'over which the advance was to take place was a far-flung plain, broken by numerous valleys, small copses, irregularly laid-out villages, and some rivers and brooks; of these the Pena ran with a swift current between steep banks. The ground rose slightly to the north, thus favouring the defence. Roads consisted of tracks through the sand and became impassable for all motor transport during rain. Large cornfields covered the landscape and made visibility difficult.'

The attack opened at 15:00 on the hot and sultry afternoon of 4 July, preceded by a short but sharp German artillery bombardment. Flanked on their left by the 48th Panzer Korps and on their right by Army Detachment 'Kempf', the SS divisions—which by this time included large numbers of the new PzKpfw V Panther tank in addition to their Tigers—made good initial progress, penetrating the positions of the 52nd Guards Rifle Division and thrusting towards Prokhorovka. On their left, 48th Panzer Korps also made good progress, but Kempf's group was seriously held up and the SS right flank was threatened. The advance continued more slowly on the 5th, the SS units heading towards Prokhorovka through the second line of Soviet defences. On the 6th, however, rain delayed the advance until mid-afternoon, and the Panzers succeeded in covering a mere twelve miles (19 km). By the 7th, after only three days' fighting, the SS Panzer Korps' original complement of 200 Panthers had been reduced to a mere forty, although they could derive a measure of grim satisfaction from the destruction of some 400 Soviet armoured fighting vehicles. (One of the reasons for the loss rate among the Panthers was the susceptibility of early production models to catching fire very easily when hit.)

The 8th and 9th saw little German progress, and on 10 July the Russians went over to the counter-offensive. The largest tank battle of World War 2, and the largest of all time until the Arab-Israeli Wars, took place on the 12th, between some 700 tanks of the SS Panzer Korps—approximately 100 of which were Tigers—and roughly 850 of the Soviet Marshal Rotmistrov's T-34s, KV-1s and -2s and other AFVs.

'By evening knocked-out tanks of both nations littered the steppes and smoke from burning machines darkened the skies above the salient,' said one eyewitness. The fighting had been intense, often at point-blank range, and both sides displayed a high

Hitler's Teutonic Knights

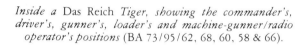

Inside a Das Reich *Tiger, showing the commander's, driver's, gunner's, loader's and machine-gunner/radio operator's positions (BA 73/95/62, 68, 60, 58 & 66).*

Left *PzKpfw III and SdKfz 251s of* Das Reich *during the battle of Kursk* (BA 73/80/40).

Below *Very clear shot of a* Das Reich *PzKpfw IVB or C moving up to the Kursk front* (BA 125/257/24).

Below right *Aboard an SdKfz 251 during the battle of Kursk* (BA 73/80/38).

degree of almost suicidal courage. But the men of Hausser's Panzer Korps proved the stronger, and in the end Rotmistrov was forced to withdraw. However, losses on both sides had been heavy—over 300 tanks each—and the Germans now lacked the strength to resume the offensive. Operation 'Zitadelle' was abandoned on 13 July and the German forces fell back on the defensive.

The deteriorating situation in Italy, where Anglo-American forces had now landed, claimed Hitler's attention at this point, and on the 17th he ordered the SS Panzer Korps out of the line to hold itself in readiness for a transfer. In the end, however, only the Leibstandarte *Adolf Hitler* was sent, as described in the previous chapter, and *Das Reich* and *Totenkopf* were left to help the Army stem the renewed Russian onslaught.

The next three months saw the German forces reeling back, often in disorder, on all fronts despite desperate delaying tactics by *Das Reich* and other crack units. Kharkov and Kiev both fell; but in November a fresh counter-attack, spearheaded by the SS divisions (including the Leibstandarte *Adolf Hitler*, hastily recalled from Italy), succeeded in checking the Soviet advance. A see-saw situation developed with both sides trying to encircle isolated groups of their opponents, sometimes successfully, at other times vainly.

In December an advance party from SS-Division *Das Reich* returned to East Prussia for the purpose of reorganizing the formation with a full complement of Panther and Tiger tanks, and in early February 1944 further elements of the division began arriving at their new training ground in Bordeaux. A battle-group, Kampfgruppe *Lammerding* (named after its commander, Oberführer Heinz Lammerding) remained in Russia, where it was caught in the Kamenets-Podolsk Pocket and formed the rearguard while other German units escaped.

In April the majority of the survivors of this action,

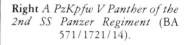

Left Das Reich *PzKpfw IV during the winter of 1943* (BA 571/1721/21).

Right *A PzKpfw V Panther of the 2nd SS Panzer Regiment* (BA 571/1721/14).

Left *PzKpfw IVs, some with and some without schürzen, and Tigers of the* Das Reich *Division* (BA 571/1721/26).

Right *More PzKpfw IVs, showing the division's special marking which was applied earlier in the year for the Kursk offensive* (BA 571/1721/21).

Hitler's Teutonic Knights

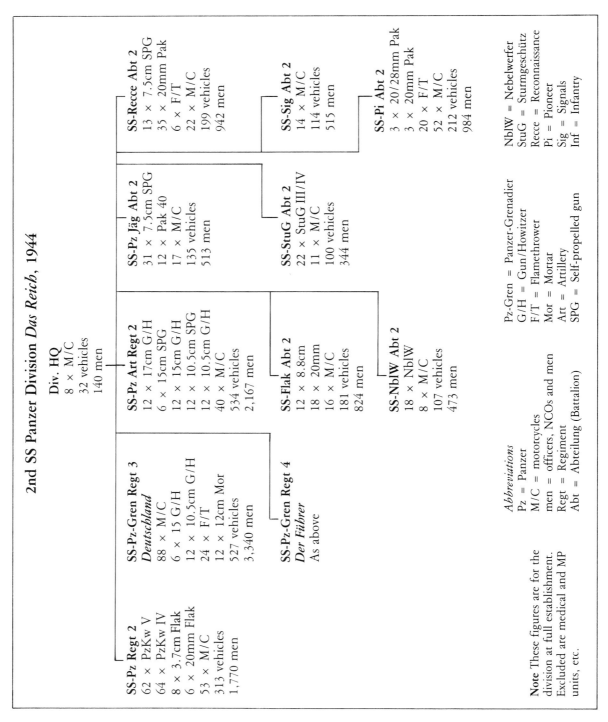

2nd SS Panzer Division *Das Reich*, 1944

Div. HQ
8 × M/C
32 vehicles
140 men

SS-Recce Abt 2
13 × 7.5cm SPG
35 × 20mm Pak
6 × F/T
22 × M/C
199 vehicles
942 men

SS-Sig Abt 2
14 × M/C
114 vehicles
515 men

SS-Pi Abt 2
3 × 20/28mm Pak
3 × 20mm Pak
20 × F/T
52 × M/C
212 vehicles
984 men

SS-Pz Jäg Abt 2
31 × 7.5cm SPG
12 × Pak 40
17 × M/C
135 vehicles
513 men

SS-StuG Abt 2
22 × StuG III/IV
11 × M/C
100 vehicles
344 men

SS-Pz Art Regt 2
12 × 17cm G/H
6 × 15cm SPG
12 × 15cm G/H
12 × 10.5cm SPG
12 × 10.5cm G/H
40 × M/C
534 vehicles
2,167 men

SS-Flak Abt 2
12 × 8.8cm
18 × 20mm
16 × M/C
181 vehicles
824 men

SS-NblW Abt 2
18 × NblW
8 × M/C
107 vehicles
473 men

SS-Pz-Gren Regt 3
Deutschland
88 × M/C
6 × 15 G/H
12 × 10.5cm G/H
24 × F/T
12 × 12cm Mor
527 vehicles
3,340 men

SS-Pz-Gren Regt 4
Der Führer
As above

SS-Pz Regt 2
62 × PzKw V
64 × PzKw IV
8 × 3.7cm Flak
6 × 20mm Flak
53 × M/C
313 vehicles
1,770 men

Abbreviations
Pz = Panzer
M/C = motorcycles
men = officers, NCOs and men
Regt = Regiment
Abt = Abteilung (Battalion)

Pz-Gren = Panzer-Grenadier
G/H = Gun/Howitzer
F/T = Flamethrower
Mor = Mortar
Art = Artillery
SPG = Self-propelled gun

NblW = Nebelwerfer
StuG = Sturmgeschütz
Recce = Reconnaissance
Pi = Pioneer
Sig = Signals
Inf = Infantry

Note These figures are for the division at full establishment. Excluded are medical and MP units, etc.

Paul Hausser flanked by General der Fallschirmjäger Meindl and General-Leutnant Schimpff (BA 586/243/7a).

fought in freezing fog, were also sent to Bordeaux, leaving just the small Kampfgruppe *Weidinger* still in the east. This unit was heavily engaged during its retreat through Proskurov and Tarnopol.

The organization of the reconstituted division can be seen in the accompanying chart (the other SS Panzer Divisions were basically the same), and it was with these forces that the division marched north in June 1944 to meet the Allied invasion in Normandy. During this operation, two incidents occurred which have severely tarnished the division's name.

Fighting its way into the little town of Tulle, which had been occupied by the French Resistance, the division's reconnaissance unit discovered the mutilated corpses of 62 German soldiers who had apparently surrendered to the partisans and been killed out of hand. In reprisal, 99 Frenchmen suspected of belonging to the Resistance were hanged. It is, perhaps, possible to justify this as a genuine act of war rather than the 'massacre of the innocents' that it has been described as elsewhere; but what followed shortly at Oradour cannot.

As the division passed close to the town, SS Sturmbannführer Helmut Kampf was abducted and killed by the French Resistance. In reprisal a company leader for *Der Führer* Regiment ordered the entire population of 642 men, women and children to be

murdered, and the town was blown up and burned to the ground. There was never any serious suggestion that any one of the villagers could have been connected with the killing of the officer; the troops who carried out the massacre were seasoned veterans; and the atrocity was committed calmly and methodically, not in a wave of battlefield hysteria. Oradour remains the most damning answer known in the West to the most frequently heard arguments of SS apologists, and is a terrible stain on the record of German arms.

Arriving in Normandy, the SS-Division *Das Reich* was thrown into the line north of St Lô, where it faced the American divisions which had landed on Omaha and Utah beaches. A series of counter-attacks failed to throw the Americans back into the sea, and, when they broke out from the beach-head at Avranches, *Das Reich* found itself encircled at Coutances. The Germans succeeded in breaking out of this trap on 29 July, however, and then captured Mortain, but had to withdraw in common with other German forces to avoid being wiped out piecemeal by the devastating Allied fighter-bomber attacks and Patton's fast-moving ground forces. The division was lucky enough to escape being trapped in the Falaise Pocket and, indeed, was largely instrumental in holding open the 24-mile (38-km) 'neck' of this pocket,

Hitler's Teutonic Knights

The havoc caused by Allied aerial bombing. This was St Lô! (BA 494/3398/27).

enabling a large number of other German troops to escape before the trap snapped shut. Retreating slowly across the River Seine in August, the division retired behind the West Wall in September.

While the Allies maintained relentless pressure on the German lines, Hitler was reorganizing his forces for one final gamble in the west—the Ardennes offensive. For this operation, 2nd SS Panzer Division *Das Reich* was seconded to 'Sepp' Dietrich's 6th SS Panzer Army, where it formed the north flank reserve. On 19 December it was transferred to von Manteuffel's 5th Panzer Army and thrust through the positions of the American 82nd Airborne Division at St Vith, pushing on to within sight of the River Meuse by Christmas. However, 101st Airborne's heroic defence at Bastogne had halted the main impetus of the German thrust, reinforcements were rushed to the threatened area by Patton in one of the most remarkable manoeuvres of the war and, worst of all, the weather abated, clear skies bringing hordes of Allied aircraft to finally break up the attack. A large part of *Das Reich* was cut off and its personnel captured by two Allied divisions at the end of the year, and the remainder retreated.

Hastily refitted once again, the division was finally sent to Hungary, where it fought a steady delaying action against the Russians, retreating slowly into Austria. It stubbornly defended Vienna until 15 April 1945 but was finally forced to evacuate. The *Der Führer* Regiment was engaged in fighting the insurrection in Prague at the beginning of May, and succeeded in getting a large part of the city's civilian population away from the Russian advance.

Germany surrendered on 7 May and the majority of *Das Reich*'s personnel entered American captivity. On 9 May, the *Deutschland* Regiment radioed the following message: 'The Regiment *Deutschland*—now completely cut-off, without supplies, with losses of seventy per cent in personnel and equipment, at the end of its strength— must capitulate. Tomorrow the Regiment will march into captivity all heads held high. The Regiment which had the honour of bearing the name *Deutschland* is now signing off.'

Paul Hausser levers himself into the turret of a Das Reich *PzKpfw III which has spare track links liberally added for extra protection* (BA 81/142/30).

3. 3rd SS Panzer Division
Totenkopf

When the often thin and hotly debated line between those men who were actively involved with the running of the Nazi concentration camps, and those who were purely front-line soldiers wearing SS rather than Army insignia, comes up for discussion, the greyest area is always the SS *Totenkopf* Division. To a degree, apologists for the Waffen-SS have done to this unit what the rest of the world did to the SS as a whole: branded it as responsible for all the worst atrocities. Similarly, those with anti-SS views tend to say, 'well, these chaps were concentration camp guards, but they were held up as an élite Waffen-SS fighting unit, so where does that leave the Leibstandarte, *Das Reich* and others?'

The facts of the matter are simple. The *Totenkopf* Division was originally created from the five pre-war Standarten responsible for guarding the concentration camps, with a leavening of properly trained soldiers from the SS-VT. Until the invasion of Russia, its personnel were still exchanged for guard duties more often than those of the SS-VT. After the invasion of Russia, there was no more interchange than in any other Waffen-SS unit, and the *Totenkopf* Division fought hard and well for almost four years, practically without respite, on the Eastern Front. It was never as well trained or, until 1943, as well equipped as the Leibstandarte or *Das Reich*; nor does it appear to have been as well motivated as *Wiking* or *Hitlerjugend*. But it made no mean showing. In 1944, General Wöhler, commander of the 8th Army, described the division as 'a lightning sword of retribution' which fulfilled its tasks with 'unshakeable fortitude'. Unfortunately, it never threw off its original reputation and, having surrendered to the Americans in Austria in May 1945, the survivors of the division were handed over to the Russians—against whom they had fought since 1941. All were executed or died in penal servitude.

In October 1939, following the Polish campaign, the Inspector of Concentration Camps, Theodor Eicke, gained permission to create an SS field division. The nucleus for this already existed in the five battalion-strength Totenkopfverbände Sturmbanne—No 1 *Oberbayern*, No 2 *Elbe*, No 3 *Sachsen*, No 4 *Ostfriedland* and No 5 *Brandenburg*, based at Dachau, Sachsenhausen, Frankenberg, Buchenwald and Mauthausen respectively—which totalled some 7,400 men. 6,500 of these were formed into three regiments with trained officers from the SS-VT; some additional experienced troops were drawn from the former Totenkopf Standarte *Götze* which had been formed for police duties in Danzig during the Polish campaign but actually found itself fighting with the Army. However, the Army was dismissive of the men of the *Totenkopf* Division, calling them policemen under arms, and to begin with refused to allow service in this division to count as genuine military service.

During the early months of 1940, Himmler and Berger began an active recruiting campaign for the *Totenkopf* as well as for the Leibstandarte and SS-VT, but there were differences between the recruiting standards. Men for the *Totenkopf* were to be aged between 17 and 26, while the other two formations accepted them only up to age 22; men for the Leibstandarte had to be at least 6 ft ½ in tall, while those for the SS-VT and *Totenkopf* had only to be 5 ft 7½ in. All, however, had to be of 'Aryan' ancestry, in good health and with clean police records.

Alongside its battle for recognition, the *Totenkopf* also had to fight for weapons and equipment, and the OKH (Army High Command) disdained even to answer a request for field and anti-tank guns. However, Hitler intervened and in March 1940 authorized the formation of an SS Artillery Regiment of three battalions, one each of which would be assigned to the Leibstandarte, the SS-VT and the Polizei Division. To get around the Army's resistance to supplying them with modern guns, the SS took over captured Czech weapons from the Skoda works.

When the *Totenkopf* Division was assigned to Max Weichs' 2nd Army for the invasion of the west, a miracle of training, organization and equipment had been achieved, and on his first inspection of the division on 4 April Weichs was considerably surprised to find that it was not 'organized and equipped like a Czech foot division' but was really a modern, motorized infantry division. The inspection altered Weichs' attitude towards the SS which had previously been hostile, not least because he was a devout Catholic. Other Army officers were later to share the same opinion of the *Totenkopf*, Manstein for example saying that 'as far as its discipline and soldierly bearing went, the division. . .undoubtedly made a good impression'. Throughout the war, Manstein continued, the *Totenkopf* 'always showed great dash in the assault and was steadfast in defence'.

At the beginning of the 1940 campaign the *Totenkopf* was held in reserve at Kassel, in Germany, but on 16 May it was ordered forward into Belgium to join 15th Panzer Korps (5th and 7th Panzer Divisions). The division reached the position held by Rommel's 7th Panzers at Le Cateau on the 19th. Here their advance had been interrupted by a British strongpoint and the *Totenkopf* got its first taste of action. In the fierce day's fighting on the 20th, *Totenkopf* lost 16 killed and 53 wounded; the next day was even tougher, but surprisingly, casualties were lower—19 killed and 27 wounded. On this occasion, the British threw 74 Matilda tanks, slow-moving but heavily armoured and impervious to all current German anti-tank guns except the dual-purpose 8.8 cm, into the assault, supported by two battalions of infantry and sixty French tanks. After their previous victories, this counter-attack came as a surprise to the Germans, but they managed to hold out and the advance continued towards the series of canal lines behind which the British had established defensive positions.

By 27 May the *Totenkopf* had reached the canal at Bethune and forced a crossing, then ploughing northwards towards Merville. Casualties, however, had been heavy, and provoked the Korps commander, General Hoeppner, into reproving Eicke with the words 'You are a butcher and no soldier'. Butchery, indeed, was to follow.

As the *Totenkopf* headed for Merville, the 4th Company of the 2nd Regiment was held up by the courageously determined resistance of a small group of about a hundred men from the 2nd Royal Norfolk Regiment. Retreating through the little hamlet of Le Paradis, the English soldiers first attempted to hold out in a farmhouse, but when this was set on fire by German mortar fire, they retreated to the shelter of a cowshed. When it became obvious to the exhausted, red-eyed British troops that further resistance was useless, they waved a white towel out of the door. The firing stopped. A Sergeant, accompanied by half a dozen men, gingerly left the cowshed. Immediately, the Germans opened fire again. 'Hands up! Hands up!', they screamed. The soldiers emerged from the cowshed with their hands on top of their heads.

After being searched, the men were marched along the lane to another farm building. Ominously, two heavy machine-guns had been set up in the field facing its long side. The prisoners were lined up against this wall and the machine-guns opened up, raking backwards and forwards into the helpless crowd. Incredibly, there were two badly wounded survivors, Privates Albert Pooley and William O'Callaghan. After the *Totenkopf* men departed, they crawled out from under the pile of bodies. Pooley later said, 'My arm was over my head and I could just look along the pile of bodies. I saw a German soldier step down into a hole with bayonet fixed. It was a terrible suspense. A bayonet is not a nice finish. Then a whistle blew and I heard an order. The man clambered out before he reached me.'

The two Privates were succoured by the villagers of Le Paradis but later gave themselves up to a regular German Army unit in order to avoid any reprisals against their helpers. Private Pooley was repatriated in 1943 as a result of his injuries, but on his return to England no-one believed his story. 'Such things only happen in Russia', they thought. It was only at the end of the war, when Private O'Callaghan independently related the same story, that the incredible truth finally emerged.

The man responsible for the atrocity was Obersturmführer Fritz Knöchlein, who had originally enlisted in the *Deutschland* Regiment of the SS-VT then been transferred as a company commander in the *Totenkopf* at Dachau concentration camp. After the war he was recognized during a search of PoW camps and arrested. At his trial in Hamburg a villager from Le Paradis, Madame Castel, positively identified him. Convicted on 25 October 1948, he

Theodore Eicke and Max Simon celebrate Christmas 1941 in a festively decorated dacha (BA 75/120/7a).

was hanged three months later.

The rest of the *Totenkopf* earned itself a better reputation that grim day of 28 May 1940, pushing back the British defenders in its path and causing 300 casualties for the loss of 150 of its own men. Shortly after Dunkirk, the division was withdrawn from the line and was then sent to follow up the Leibstandarte's headlong advance through France, ending the campaign victoriously in Boulogne. The *Totenkopf*'s only real battle in France was at Tarare, on the approach to Lyon, where its reconnaissance battalion fought a short, sharp engagement with some French colonial troops and took 6,000 prisoners.

During the early months of 1941, the strength of the *Totenkopf* Division was rapidly increased by the devious machinations of Gottlob Berger. In June 1940 it had been 20,000-strong. Of these, however, 13,246 were over-age reservists. By the same time the next year there were 40,000 men in the *Totenkopf*

Totenkopf *troops during the advance into Russia.* **Left** *Theodore Eicke confers with Richard Pauli and other officers.* **Above** *Pak 35/36 in action* (Left, BA 78/22/8; above, Christopher Ailsby Historical Archives).

Division and the seventeen *Totenkopf* Standarten. The latter were assigned occupation duties in Norway, France and elsewhere and largely comprised the older men, while the younger and fitter were assigned to the field division. Three Standarten were, however, later given field duties for the Russian campaign, two of them forming Kampfgruppe *Nord*, which disgraced itself in its first battle. The third was attached to *Reich* for the Balkan campaign and did not distinguish itself either.

At the beginning of Operation 'Barbarossa' the *Totenkopf* Division consisted of 18,754 men organized as a proper motorized infantry division with three regiments as before plus full supporting reconnaissance, anti-tank and artillery formations, etc. In June 1941 the division was assigned to von Leeb's Army Group North whose principal objective was Leningrad. To begin with they made sweeping progress through Lithuania, whose inhabitants hailed the Germans as liberators: in fact, many men from the Baltic states, relieved of the Russian yoke, would flock to join the Waffen-SS, and would later constitute three full fighting divisions. By the end of

June *Totenkopf* had reached the River Dvina and the Army Group had destroyed an estimated twelve to fifteen Soviet divisions in the process. By the middle of July it had penetrated into Russia proper and reached Pskov. But Russian resistance was getting stronger, and the countryside was becoming more marshy and densely forested as the German forces approached the Russian 'lake district'.

Towards the end of August a final drive towards Leningrad began, with the Finns closing in on the city from the north, and by 31 August German armoured spearheads were within ten miles (16 km) of the city outskirts. On 8 September they had reached Lake Ladoga, completing an encirclement of Leningrad. Now, however, Hitler needed Manstein's and Reinhardt's Panzer divisions for Operation 'Taifun', the assault on Moscow, and they were switched to the central front, leaving *Totenkopf*, the 4th SS Polizei Division and various Army infantry divisions to invest the city and, hopefully, starve the defenders into submission.

During October the SS tightened their grip on the city and even pushed east as far as Tikhvin, but the

division was forced back to a line along the River Volkhov by Russian counter-attacks in December. And here, to all intents and purposes, it was to remain until 1942. Leningrad never succumbed. To get supplies into the city the ingenious Russians built roads across the frozen surface of Lake Ladoga during the winters of 1940-41 and 1941-42, and even a single-track railway line! The population of the city suffered some of the worst privations of the whole war, being subjected to cold, starvation and disease; to eating rats and to tearing up railway sleepers for firewood. But they did not give in, and the defence of Leningrad remains one of the most incredible feats of human endurance in the annals of warfare.

It was not the sort of warfare that the men of the *Totenkopf* had hoped for, and as they shivered in their dug-outs through that first bitter winter many of them must have wondered what they had signed up for. Things became even worse as the Russians broke through in between Army Groups North and Centre, trying to encircle the latter and forcing the Germans to pull back to a defensive line some 85 miles (136 km) west of Moscow. This left the *Totenkopf* itself practically surrounded in the Demyansk area, a form of stalemate situation which essentially lasted throughout 1942 while German forces swept forward to the Caucasus in the south. In January the division was completely encircled and heavy fighting continued until April, when it succeeded in breaking out to the north-west. *Totenkopf* was then purely on the defensive for six months until it was pulled out of the line, having lost some sixty per cent of its original strength, in October. Between then and February 1943 it enjoyed a rest in France, was brought back up to strength and re-equipped as a Panzergrenadier division.

In March 1943 it followed the Leibstandarte and *Das Reich* back to Russia, taking part in the major battles for Kharkov and Kursk, which have been described in Chapters 1 and 2, as part of Hausser's 1st

Left *Dug-in on the icy perimeter of Leningrad* (BA 214/313/12).

Above *StuG IIIs of the* Totenkopf *Division during the spring thaw* (BA 81/143/25a).

Below *One of the division's PzKpfw IIIs at Lushna during 1942* (BA 75/118/8).

Background photograph *A flare illuminates a* Totenkopf *patrol on the fringe of a wood.*
Inset Totenkopf *anti-tank gunners in winter camouflage with a 3.7 cm Pak 35/36 (BA 77/93/5 & 78/22/16).*

PzKpfw IIIs, IVs and VIs, plus a StuG III, of the Totenkopf Division *during the fierce fighting for Kharkov in March/April 1943 (BA 78/22/17, 81/142/33, 73/113/18 & 73/89/58).*

Hitler's Teutonic Knights

Left *Brief respite for the crew of a* Totenkopf *PzKpfw IV during the battle of Kursk* (BA 78/22/23).

Left *First aid for a lightly wounded grenadier of the* Totenkopf *Division* (BA 78/22/21).

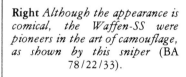

Right *Although the appearance is comical, the Waffen-SS were pioneers in the art of camouflage, as shown by this sniper* (BA 78/22/33).

Left Totenkopf *gunners with a 5 cm Pak 38 during the battle of Kursk. Note 'kill' markings on barrel* (BA 73/85/36).

Left *Good portrait shot of a* Totenkopf *tank commander in 1944 (BA 695/406/16a).*

Below left *An Oberleutnant of the 228th Infantry Regiment confers with a bespectacled Untersturmführer of the* Totenkopf *Division (BA 24/3535/32).*

Below right *Loading the 1,000th shell into the breech of an SS 10.5 cm leFH 18 (BA 73/92/46).*

Right and below far right *Divisional insignia were rarely applied to Panthers, but these two* Totenkopf *vehicles are obvious exceptions (BA 695/419/2a & 3a).*

Panzer Korps. During this period, the three principal regiments of the division received names as well as numbers. In recognition of their service, Hitler decreed that the 1st SS-T (Infanterie) Regiment should itself bear the name 'Totenkopf'; the 2nd would henceforth be named 'Thule', while the 3rd, in honour of the divisional commander—who had been killed on 28 February 1943 when his Fieseler Storch was shot down by a Russian fighter— would be called 'Theodor Eicke'.

During that long, hot summer and autumn of 1943, the *Totenkopf* Division was constantly on the defensive, retreating reluctantly and stubbornly, but retreating nonetheless. Back through Kharkov to the line of the River Dnieper, then to Stalino and Krivoi-Rog at the turn of the year. Again the division was on the defensive—that most difficult of all military operations—but it fulfilled its role admirably. After the awful winter of 1943-44, when the Russians were rolling up everything before them, the division was briefly transferred to the central sector of the front, where it encountered heavy fighting around Grodno, before it was moved further north and, in

This photograph Totenkopf *grenadier just having discharged a grenade from his rifle attachment. Right* Tiger *and* PzKpfw IVH *of the* Totenkopf *Division late in 1944* (BA 695/406/15a & 2a).

common with *Wiking*, was in the front line holding back the Soviet advance into Poland in the Bialystock region.

At the end of 1944 the division was sent, with *Wiking* again (see Chapter 4), to attempt the relief of German troops cut off by the advancing Red Army in Budapest. After this failed, the division retreated into Austria where, as related at the beginning of this chapter, it surrendered to the American Army. The final survivors, a mere thousand men and six tanks from what had been one of the SS's premier divisions, were handed over to the Russians. Despite its faltering beginnings and the unquestioned guilt of the Le Paradis massacre, it was a sad fate for a division whose fighting record qualifies it for the appelation 'élite' in any military history.

SS Grenadiers wait for a Soviet artillery barrage to lift (BA 81/142/13).

4. 5th SS Panzer Division
Wiking

In their post-war writings and speeches, both Gott-lob Berger and Felix Steiner argued that, in recruiting men into the Waffen-SS from the occupied countries of Europe, they were engaged not only in a crusade against communism but also in taking the first steps towards a European union with Germans and others working together in a common cause. The *Wiking* Division, which was formed initially of predominantly Dutch and Danish volunteers around a cadre of experienced German soldiers, has often been held up as the prime example of this concept in action, and has even been claimed as a forerunner of NATO. One Dutch ex-SS NCO, who surrendered to the Americans (along with the bulk of the division) in May 1945, told me that the western European volunteers were separated from their German comrades in a special camp where they were allowed to retain all their badges, medals and papers and even their weapons, although no ammunition. Since it has long been widely known—even though officially denied—that many Allied officers, and not just the vociferous General George Patton, felt that the advance should have been continued into Russia after the collapse of Germany, the obvious conclusion is that these men would have been recruited into the Allied army. If such is the case, the full facts are unlikely to emerge until the middle of the next century—possibly never.

In December 1940, as Gottlob Berger's recruiting campaign gathered momentum, the *Germania* Regiment of the SS-VT Division was nominated as the cadre unit of a new division to be recruited as much as possible from the occupied countries of Europe. Already in existence were the Scandinavian Standarte *Nordland*, raised earlier in the year and comprising 294 Norwegians and 216 Danes; and the Standarte *Westland* whose strength stood at 630 Dutch and Flemish volunteers. The motivation of those early non-German recruits is one which provokes endless argument. Later in the war, after the German invasion of the Soviet Union, large numbers of men volunteered, not because they had fascist political tendencies or because they were particularly pro-German, but because they genuinely believed in the cause of fighting communism. Other reasons, particularly by about 1943, included war privations at home which led many to believe that they would be better off in the Waffen-SS. At the beginning, however, it seems to have been more a simple desire for adventure. As George Stein has observed, the sweeping German military successes could not fail to impress, and there was a temptation to put the blame for defeat on the home government rather than on the Germans. Moreover, the military bearing and conduct of German soldiery in the occupied countries was exemplary in those early months, before the witch-hunt for Jews to send to forced labour and, later, extermination camps, gained full strength, and before the growth in resistance movements forced the occupying power to adopt harsher attitudes. Certainly, among the early volunteers there appears to have been little political motivation. The reason for this is that the leaders of the non-German fascist parties, such as Mussert in Holland, Dégrelle in Belgium and Quisling in Norway, resisted recruit-

Left A Wiking *NCO gives the order to advance.* **Above** *Norwegian volunteers are sworn in* (BA 70/25/6 & 81/148/11).

ment of their members into the German forces unless they could be commanded by their own officers. This opposition did not, however, last long under pressure from the energetic Gottlob Berger.

The first commander of the new division was Felix Steiner who, as described in *Hitler's Samurai*, was a first-class officer with a number of innovative ideas. He was no Nazi, although his experiences in Russia were later to turn him into a fervent opponent of communism, and he remained an active member of the Protestant church throughout. This, and his outspoken attitudes towards the way the war should be run, often brought him into conflict with the German high command, but his service record made him too valuable to replace.

Within the Waffen-SS there had existed from the outset a much closer camaraderie between officers and men than was possible within the Wehrmacht, and this was something which Steiner approved of and did his utmost to foster in his new division. Securing the right balance between informality and military discipline is something like tightrope-walking in the best of circumstances, and Steiner's problem was exacerbated by the mixture of

Germans, Dutch, Danes, Flemings, Walloons, Norwegians and, for a while, Finns whom he had to command. To what extent he succeeded is described by the German Army Chaplain, Kapitän Rev Karl Ossenkop, who was seconded to the 3rd (Germanic) Panzer Korps in 1944. 'The particular impression I received—after I had got to know during the course of the war a great many Divisions and Korps—was an excellent spirit of comradeship. In contrast to Army units, differences in rank did not constitute boundaries between one man and another. There were no pedantic forms which had anxiously to be maintained. This did not lead to disorderly ways, but to a voluntary discipline of a kind which I have seldom experienced. There was no force, let alone terror. . . Nor have I ever known a unit in which members criticized as freely and openly the government and the Party. Because of that I, too, had the opportunity to speak openly.'

However, such comradeship and freedom of expression did not arise naturally. It had to be cultivated and, until the division had been welded into one during its long march across Russia to the Caucasus Mountains, there were rumblings of discontent among the western European volunteers. Having been promised identical consideration and treatment to that experienced by any German SS soldier, many of them found the reality rather different. Although Steiner himself actively stamped on discrimination wherever he found it, many of his officers—particularly those who had served in the Army before transferring to the Waffen-SS—found the mental adjustment difficult. Complaints about treatment by German officers and instructors of the 'ethnic' volunteers became rife. Poorer rations, docked pay for imaginary misdemeanours, extra duties and less leave were among the principal complaints, many of them fully justified, nor did they disappear once the division went into combat and at last, in January 1942, Steiner was forced to take the exceptional step of issuing the following order to his officers.

'More than any other unit, this division must ensure that the task of leadership is carried out in the right manner. In view of the diverse origins of the replacement troops [ie, newly arrived volunteers] a spirit of comradeship can grow only slowly, and mistakes made in the process can have more serious consequences than among Reichsdeutsche troops. The most important precondition for a humane

leadership is the incessant and continuous care of the superior for his subordinates. He must see that his subordinates place their fullest confidence in him in the knowledge that he is their best comrade.

'The troops ought to worship him. Every superior must therefore closely identify himself with his unit. Platoon and Company commanders especially must be in continuous, intimate contact with their soldiers. They must be an example and have their confidence in all matters. . .

'The more reasonably, thoughtfully and sympathetically a unit is led, the stronger is its cohesion and the greater its combat value. Especially because of our Nordic volunteers, a humane leadership seems to me to be of decisive importance. I therefore ask all superior officers to endeavour seriously and

Below left *SS radio operator in Russia.*
Below right *Column of SS trucks during the advance.*
Below far right Wiking *Division SdKfz 232* (BA 73/82/37, 75/120/34a & 73/87/32).

Hitler's Teutonic Knights

continuously to create close human relationships in their units. The task of the Division will be eased decisively through this and carried out by everyone—superiors and subordinates alike—with greater dedication.'

That Steiner's order, and his continuing concern for his men, were eventually to work is shown in Kapitän Ossenkop's earlier remarks. Moreover, the division's fighting ability—particularly after it was re-formed as a Panzergrenadier Division in November 1942—became second to none, and Russian officers would heave a sigh of relief when *Wiking* was withdrawn from the line for a rest. The commander of the 27th Army Corps, Major-General Artemko, said after he had been captured that the military performance of the division surpassed anything he had experienced before, and that the units under his command were always relieved when it was replaced by a Wehrmacht unit! However, *Wiking* suffered the penalty for its ferocious reputation: following its failure in one operation, a footnote to the OKW (Oberkommando der Wehrmacht) records com-

ments that things had gone wrong not because of lack of fighting spirit but because 'so many officers had been killed that there were no longer sufficient with command of the necessary languages'. Gerald Reitlinger offers a further explanation for the fighting spirit of the European volunteers, commenting that: 'to the German soldier, surrender meant a prisoner-of-war camp, but to the foreign collaborator it might well mean the firing squad'.

Steiner's new division first saw action during the invasion of Russia in June 1941, although the *Germania* Regiment had, of course, taken part in the invasion of France the previous year as part of the SS-VT Division. Following its formal constitution on 1 December 1940, the division was for a brief period of three weeks known as *Germania*, but this was altered to *Wiking* in order to reflect its mixed Nordic composition and make the foreign volunteers feel more 'at home'. In June 1941 it was constituted as a motorized infantry formation with three regiments (*Germania, Nordland* and *Westland*) plus an

artillery regiment and reconnaissance, anti-tank, signals and engineering battalions in the front line, staff and supporting troops. Total strength was 19,377 men*, of whom only a third at this time were non-German volunteers. Four hundred of these were Finns, Finland being an ally rather than a vassal state; their number would swell to over a thousand before the end of the year, and they would fight with distinction until 1943, when Finland pulled out of the war.

For Operation 'Barbarossa', the 5th SS (mot) Division *Wiking* was attached to Army Group South which encountered far stiffer resistance than those of the Centre or North since Stalin had erroneously decided that the main German thrust would be made in this direction rather than towards Moscow. The Army Group had only one comparatively small Panzer Gruppe, commanded by von Kleist, which made its task even more difficult, and progress was slow until Hitler diverted Guderian's Panzer Gruppe from the central force later in the summer to help in the mass encirclement battles which reaped such a rich harvest of prisoners but which proved ultimately to have been a strategic disaster.

During the first months of the campaign Steiner's division moved forward decisively from its assembly area at Cholm through Lemberg and Tarnopol to Zhitomir by mid-July then to Byela Tserkov Usin at the end of the month where, with 3rd Panzer Korps, it helped complete the encirclement of Russian forces in the Uman pocket on 3 August. This was finally destroyed on the 9th and *Wiking* pushed on to Dnepropetrovsk where it overcame stiff opposition at the end of the month. As in France in 1940, the blitzkrieg appeared unstoppable as the division pressed onwards across the steppes, the main adversaries being the intense heat and the fine dust which pervaded everything, clogging tank engines as well as the men's noses and throats. Past Cherkassy, later to be the scene of the division's single most notable achievement, Army Group South pressed onwards, encountering stiff resistance at Dnepropetrovsk, on the River Dnieper. However, a crossing was forced and *Wiking* continued eastward towards Schalty

*19,021 according to some sources.

while other units of the Army Group battled down the strong Russian defences in the Crimea, past Stalino and finally to their first main objective of the campaign, Rostov-on-Don. Here, in November 1941, however, the triumphant advance came to a halt. In the north, Leningrad was besieged but would hold out; in the centre, the stubborn defenders of Moscow, aided by the appalling weather which had done so much to slow the German advance, dug in and waited for a final assault which never came; and in the south, having travelled further in five short months than any army before them, both men and machinery were worn out. On all three fronts, therefore, the Germans paused to regroup, consolidate their positions and await the inevitable Russian counter-attack.

During December 1941-February 1942 the German defenders gave ground grudgingly. At this period of the war the Soviet tactics lacked sophistication, but this was more than compensated for by sheer weight of numbers. The *Wiking* Division was forced out of the Alexejevka area, where the fighting had been particularly bitter, into defensive positions behind the River Msus. Against the Russian threat the Germans utilized what are knows as 'hedgehog' tactics: instead of trying to maintain a continuous line, the major units were formed into approximately circular perimeters for all-round defence. When the Russians attacked, they would penetrate the 'soft' zones in between these perimeters and leave themselves wide open for strong counter-attacks into their flanks. It was during this period that, says George Stein, the 'Waffen-SS displayed what was for Hitler to become its greatest virtue: the ability to retain its fighting spirit even in defeat. It was this quality that led Hitler to order an expansion of the Waffen-SS towards the end of 1942.'

This expansion was not approved of by all. General Siegfried Westphal, in *The Fatal Decisions* (Consul Books, Manchester, 1965), wrote as follows. 'On the Eastern Front, during the early months of 1942 when the Soviet offensive had at last been

Right *PzKpfw III in whitewash camouflage for the Russian winter.* **Overleaf** *PzKpfw III and infantry in November 1941* (BPK WII140 F 3287c & WII139 F 3279b).

Hitler's Teutonic Knights

halted, the German Army faced the task of clearing up the many enemy salients which had been driven through our lines and in breaking the numerous Russian encirclements which had cut off smaller or larger bodies of our troops. The most important of these operations were directed against the encirclements of Cholm and Demyansk, the deep salient towards Isyum, south of Kharkov, and the Russian beach-head at Feodosia in the Crimea. Measures could also now be taken to sort out the formations which had become hopelessly entangled during the winter battle, to rest them, and to form new divisions in Germany. The Waffen-SS was expanded still further which was to the disadvantage of the Army whose battle-tried divisions were thus deprived of many irreplaceable junior officers and senior non-commissioned officers.'

However, Westphal was at least impartial, because he voiced a similar criticism of Göring's creation of sixteen Luftwaffe field divisions, while other Army commanders, including Guderian, had nothing but praise for the conduct of the Waffen-SS during the fierce winter fighting. Stein, again, comments that 'While many Army units and their commanders panicked in the face of the unexpected Russian onslaught, the Waffen-SS stood firm. And Goebbels noted in his diary that ''if we had twenty men like ['Sepp' Dietrich] we wouldn't have to worry at all about the Eastern Front''.'

While the Leibstandarte *Adolf Hitler, Das Reich*

Left and below *PzKpfw IIIs and IVs in Russia* (BPK WII140 F 3285 & BA 215/358/32).

The destruction of Soviet armour was massive. **From left to right** *A T-28 multi-turreted tank, a T-34 and a BT-7* (BA 209/94/5, 217/485/20 8 209/56/27).

and *Totenkopf* Divisions were withdrawn to the west to be brought back up to strength and re-equipped as Panzergrenadier Divisions during 1942, *Wiking* remained very much in the front line, although reinforced by a new tank regiment—the 5th SS Panzer Regiment under the command of Sturmbannführer Johannes-Rudolf Mühlenkamp, which was formed at Sennelager on 20 April 1942. It joined the rest of the division at the beginning of May and spearheaded the new German offensive, helping capture Rostov and, with the 13th Panzer and 125th Infantry Divisions, thrusting towards the Caucasus Mountains and the Maikop oilfields which Hitler had made his principal objective for 1942, for by this time Germany was beginning to run desperately short of oil to fuel both industry and the war machine.

By early August, the division had reached the oilfields and later in the same month German troops scaled Mount Elbrus, highest pinnacle of the Caucasus, to plant their flag there, but both proved hollow victories because the industrial city of Stalingrad still held out. In another theatre of war, Mountbatten's troops landed at Dieppe to provide a foretaste of what was to follow.

At this moment, the outcome of the war hung in the balance. The Germans had taken the Mediterranean island of Crete but had failed to follow through with either an airborne or amphibious landing on Malta. Rommel and the vaunted Afrika Korps were at bay. Europe was subdued but not silent. Russia was stricken but not defeated. German lines were perilously extended, with vulnerable flanks; at home, rationing was beginning to be felt, with meat in particular scarce, and the Allied bombing offensive was slowly but surely taking its toll. Manpower for the factories was becoming difficult to find, and the forced labour contingents of 'undesirables' from the occupied countries were on the increase.

Now, however, came the disaster of the 6th Army at Stalingrad as, with the onset of another winter, the Russian Army came into its element. To the south of the beleaguered city, *Wiking* and the other divisions in the Caucasus were in grave danger of being pinned against the Black Sea coast and were forced to withdraw northwards, and *Wiking* eventually found itself once more back in Rostov. At this time, in November, if the 6th Army's commander, von Paulus, had been allowed by Hitler to retreat, a link-up with the divisions (including *Wiking,* which was designated a Panzergrenadier division on 9 November) under Manstein's control would still have been possible. A sortie was, in fact, made towards Stalingrad from the south-west, but von Paulus refused to disobey his Führer's orders and retreat. Then, under continuing Russian pressure, the Italian 8th Army which had been protecting Manstein's flank collapsed and there was no alternative for him but to pull back towards the Donets basin.

For a time, *Wiking* was moved south, to help contain a Russian thrust towards the Crimea which got almost as far as Dnepropetrovsk. Kharkov now became the centre of attention as the depleted German forces tried to hold on in the face of bitter cold, constant mechanical breakdowns, inadequate supplies and constant harassment by Russian partisans, the spectre of a second Stalingrad constantly before them. However, as described elsewhere, Hausser's new SS Panzer Korps, comprising the Leibstandarte *Adolf Hitler*, *Das Reich* and *Totenkopf,* now returned to the Eastern Front after their refit, fresh and strongly equipped with new tanks, and the Russian offensive was contained. *Wiking,* as part of 40 Panzer Korps, played a significant part in the destruction of Popov's Army Group. There were now some changes within *Wiking*. In March 1943 the Scandinavian Regiment *Nordland* was detached to form the nucleus of a new SS division, the 11th SS Freiwilligen Panzergrenadier Division *Nordland;* the independent Finnische Freiwilligen Bataillon, which had been attached to *Wiking* during 1942, was withdrawn at the request of the

Background photograph *PzKpfw IIIs of the* Wiking *Division in Russia.*
Inset left *Johannes Mühlenkamp, commander of 5 SS Panzer Regiment.*
Inset right *Men of the* Germania *Regiment crossing a river with a Pak 38* (BA 81/144/19a, 20a & 75/118/28).

Finnish government, to compensate for which *Wiking* was reinforced by an Estonian battalion and fresh Dutch and Belgian volunteers as well as by men from the latest class of German recruits.

Following the failure of the Kursk offensive in the summer of 1943, the German Army was forced on to the defensive, and *Wiking* continued to justify its fighting reputation by holding on tenaciously and yielding ground only when absolutely necessary to avoid encirclement. As winter clamped down again, 'the fighting had to be waged while mud snatched greedily at boots and insinuated itself into the tracks of the armour.

'By some miracle, 5th SS Panzer Grenadier Division managed to struggle through the black obscenity, but at the pitiful speed of no more than two or three miles an hour. The demands on the precious fuel were ruinous and, to make matters worse, the frost returned. Out came the blow-torches to free the tanks that were stuck like insects on fly paper.'[*]

By this time the Russians were breaking through the German lines everywhere, despite the heroism of the defence. A great hole was punched in Army Group Centre and part of the Soviet Army swung south, retaking Kiev and reaching Zhitomir. *Wiking,* together with Dégrelle's SS Sturm brigade *Wallonien,* was trapped at Cherkassy by Vatutin's 1st and Koniev's 2nd Ukrainian Fronts. In one of the most outstanding triumphs of determination over adversity in the annals of the war, *Wiking* punched a hole westwards through the overpowering Soviet forces while *Wallonien* guarded their rear. However, the price was heavy. Of 56,000 men trapped in the pocket, only 35,000 escaped, and *Wiking* lost all of its armour and most of its other heavy equipment. The battle had taken place in bitter cold, with freezing fog, and the pitiable survivors were in no fit state for any more. Gruppenführer Gille, who had taken over command of the division from Felix Steiner in May 1943, was forced to report to Hitler that, to all intents and purposes, the proud division had ceased to exist.

The survivors were withdrawn to Cholm to recuperate and be re-equipped, only a nucleus of

[*]Rupert Butler, *The Black Angels* (Hamlyn, 1978).

Wiking *Division PzKpfw III after leaving a Russian village on fire* (BA 78/21/3a).

Right Wiking *Division Panthers during the heavy fighting around Warsaw in late 1944. The rather crude camouflage is probably brown over the basic dark yellow* (BA 695/420/15 & 73/103/70).

some 4,000 men remaining in Russia as a small battlegroup. The reconstituted but considerably weakened division next saw action in July 1944, being sent to help bolster the Vistula front in Poland, where it remained for the rest of the year, seeing bitter fighting in the Bialystock region to the east of Warsaw. The division was not—thankfully, for the sake of its honour—involved in the suppression of the Warsaw uprising, and its last major operation showed the élan which characterized all its campaigns, even if it was doomed to failure.

By the end of 1944 the Russian advance had carried them into Hungary and the 9th SS Korps, including *Florian Geyer* and *Maria Theresia*, were trapped in Budapest. On Christmas Eve, 1944, Hitler ordered Gille's 4th SS Panzer Korps, comprising *Wiking,* now commanded by Johannes Mühlenkamp, and *Totenkopf,* to their rescue. The attack was scheduled to begin on New Year's Day. Hitler had great hopes for its success but Guderian, who had been present when the order was given, was sceptical 'since very little time had been allowed for its preparation and neither the troops nor the commanders possessed the same drive as in the old

days'. Despite these misgivings, the initial stages of the offensive went well and by 11 January *Wiking* was on the verge of recapturing Budapest airport. For the 45,000 German soldiers trapped in the city, relief looked imminent.

It was not to be. General Balck, commander of the 4th Army, saw an opportunity to entrap ten Russian divisions north of Lake Balaton, and ordered Gille's two SS divisions to his assistance. However, this operation proved too costly in the face of ever-stiffening Russian resistance and had to be called off. By this time it was too late for the defenders of Budapest, who were overwhelmed, only 785 men succeeding in escaping; *Florian Geyer* was reduced to 170 men. *Wiking* continued a stubborn but hopeless fighting retreat, the bulk of the division falling back into Czechoslovakia where they finally surrendered at Fürstenfeld, the 5th SS Panzer Regiment through Austria into southern Germany where its men dispersed, mainly into American captivity. A number, however, succeeded in evading capture and several of these enlisted in the French Foreign Legion, which asks no questions of a man's past, and continued to serve with distinction in Indo-China.

Background photograph *Nebelwerfers in action in war-torn Warsaw* (BA 696/426/20).

Inset Wiking *Division grenadiers in the Warsaw area, late 1944* (BA 696/426/22).

Left Wiking *Division StuG III on its way from Warsaw to Budapest in 1945* (BA 70/25/4).

Right *StuG IIIs and grenadiers late in the war* (BA 81/143/22a).

Below *A* Wiking *Panther during the winter of 1944* (BA 90/3918/11).

Below right *Knocked-out* Wiking *SdKfz 251 at the end of the war* (Tass).

5. 9th SS Panzer Division
Hohenstaufen

Following the generally excellent performance of the Waffen-SS in Russia during 1941-42, in December 1942 Hitler authorized the formation of two new divisions which would become the 9th, *Hohenstaufen*, and the 10th, *Frundsberg*. Unfortunately, by this time the flow of pure German volunteers for the Waffen-SS had dried up, and Himmler had to resort to conscription, largely through the Reich Labour Service. This provoked a storm of protest, not just from parents but also from church leaders and other civilian dignitaries, and forced Hans Jüttner, head of the SS-Führungshauptamt, to offer a compromise. The conscripts, mainly eighteen-year-olds, were to receive two months' basic training. At the end of that time they were to be offered a free choice as to whether they wished to stay in the Waffen-SS or leave. How true it is will probably never be proven, but at the end of this period Jüttner reported that only three of the conscripts asked to leave: one suspects some 'ballot rigging' although, of course, during their first two months' training life was probably made as easy as possible for the conscripts and emphasis would have been placed on the positive assets of belonging to the SS, rather than on the increasingly desperate situation in Russia.

Hohenstaufen, under the command of Wilhelm Bittrich, spent the whole of 1943 working up and was finally sent into action for the first time at Tarnopol in April 1944, its task—alongside *Frundsberg*, as

Left Wearing sheepskin jackets against the cold, an SS crew mans a whitewashed '88 (BPK WII161b).

Paul Hausser's new 1st SS Panzer Korps — being to stem the renewed Russian advance and rescue the Leibstandarte and other units trapped in the Kamenets-Podolsk pocket. The new and untried divisions, according to Stein, 'quickly launched a flank attack which neatly amputated the tip of the Soviet spearhead', allowing the encircled German units to break out.

When the Allies landed in Normandy on 6 June 1944, *Hohenstaufen* and *Frundsberg* were hastily recalled from Poland to the west, adding their weight to that of the Leibstandarte, *Das Reich*, *Hitlerjugend* and *Götze von Berlichingen* (see Chapter 8) in the vain attempt to prevent the American breakout at Avranches. Like the other divisions, *Hohenstaufen* suffered heavily in the desperate fighting, being hammered from the air by Allied fighter-bombers, and was forced to retreat via Rouen into Belgium, where it was briefly stationed in Brussels, then back into Holland where it was put into a rest area just outside Arnhem.

By the end of September, the advancing British 2nd Army had crossed the River Seine, passed through Brussels and penetrated into Holland. Now it faced a stern task because the next obstacle before Germany itself was the strongly defended Siegfried Line, whose northern end rested in the Reichwald just east of Nijmegen and south-east of Arnhem. Beyond this were the three river lines, the Maas, Waal and Lower Rhine. Montgomery's bold plan to break through these defences was a daylight airborne assault designed to capture the critical bridges at Nijmegen and Arnhem. The forces selected to seize

Left, right and below Hohenstaufen *Division Hummels on their way to the front* (BA 297/1708/3a, 297/1707/32 & 297/1708/12).

Overleaf *SS Schwimmwagen on the Russian steppes* (BA 81/144/8a)

the latter objective were the British 1st and 4th Parachute Brigades and the 1st Polish Parachute Brigade, which were to land to the west and south of the town. What Allied intelligence had failed to discover was the presence of the two SS divisions—however depleted after their operations in France—outside Arnhem.

The fierce battle for Arnhem has passed into military legend. It was fought with courage and chivalry by both sides. At one point, Wilhelm Bittrich invited the British paratroops to surrender. After bringing up a loudspeaker, he first played jazz records then urged the defenders of the bridgehead to 'remember your wives and sweethearts at home'. He then reeled off a list of officers already captured and promised that an entire Panzer division would be thrown against the paras unless they gave up the unequal struggle. Predictably, the response was jeers and a burst from a Bren gun.

There were pauses in the battle which were strange to SS men who had fought in Russia— temporary ceasefires while British wounded were surrendered into SS medical care. Throughout, the men of *Hohenstaufen* and *Frundsberg* behaved with punctilious correctness. There was to be no repetition of Le Paradis or Oradour to sully their names. In the St Elizabeth hospital, British surgeons worked on the wounded of both sides while SS soldiers watched and offered help. After their final and inevitable capitulation, however, the paras received worse treatment from *Totenkopf* Standarten guards escorting them back to Germany: no food or medical treatment for 48 hours, and hails of blows for prisoners who could not keep up during their fifteen-day march into captivity. The two sides of the SS were ever-present.

Hohenstaufen was retired to Germany in December 1944 in order to take part in the Ardennes offensive. As part of the 6th SS Panzer Army, its advance was delayed by the bad roads described earlier, and it was finally detached, along with *Das Reich*, to act with Manteuffel's 5th Army. The division thus acted on the northern flank of the unsuccessful operation to capture St Vith—along with Bastogne, the classic battle of the campaign—and then followed up Peiper's advance (described in Chapter 1) to Stavelot, whence it was forced to retreat by Patton's advancing forces.

Withdrawn from the battle to Germany, *Hohenstaufen* was finally thrown in alongside so many other crack divisions for the abortive relief of Budapest; falling back in face of the irresistible Russian onslaught, it finally surrendered to US troops at Steyr in Austria.

6. 10th SS Panzer Division
Frundsberg

As the 'twin' of *Hohenstaufen*, the history of the 10th SS Panzer Division, commanded by Brigadeführer Debes until it had finished training and subsequently by Gruppenführer von Treuenfeld, has already been told in the previous chapter, up to the battle of Arnhem. While *Hohenstaufen* then stayed in the west to take part in the 'battle of the bulge', *Frundsberg* was moved to the Aachen region of Germany as another pawn in the defence against the inexorable Russian hordes. Fighting on the upper Rhine, in the dense Hagenauer Forest near Strasbourg, the division equalled its 'twin's' fighting record. It was then pulled back during the final weeks of fighting in Pomerania and was eventually forced to surrender to the Soviet Army at Schönau in May 1945.

Sic transit gloria.

7. 12th SS Panzer Division
Hitlerjugend

'Taught to be fighters, not soldiers,' is how one historian has described the seventeen- and eighteen-year-olds of the Waffen-SS's last, and in many ways most meritorious, Panzer division. They employed teenage tactics: they dressed outlandishly in 'leathers'—U-boat crew clothing—and they painted their girlfriends' names shamelessly all over their tanks rather than the authorized tactical and divisional insignia. They also fought with teenage conviction and passion and introduced a deep rivalry between themselves and the veterans of the Leibstandarte by using the key symbol crossed with a runic 'S' as their divisional symbol.

The idea for a hand-picked division plucked from the flower of German youth—the Hitler Jugend organization which gave the division its name—originated with Arthur Axmann, the Hitler Youth leader, in January 1943. Gottlob Berger, responsible for so much SS recruitment, was so entranced by the scheme that he asked to be appointed the division's commander; Himmler, in one of his wiser moments, told the bureaucrat that he was far too valuable in his present position and instead picked the veteran Leibstandarte regimental commander Fritz Witt. Divisional headquarters were etablished at Beverloo in Belgium, and by the middle of the year the first 10,000 volunteers were under intensive training.

When questioned by Hitler about the new formation, Himmler confessed somewhat proudly that the average age was only eighteen. This elicited Hitler's firm approval: German youth, he said, fights 'magnificently and with incredible bravery. . .the

youngsters who come from the Hitler Youth are fanatical fighters. . . these young German lads, some only sixteen years old. . .fight more fanatically than their older comrades.'

The division was officially called into being on 24 June 1943 and after training was initially posted to France in April 1944; at the time of the Allied invasion on 6 June it was stationed just south of Paris and was thus in an ideal position to start the counter-offensive. The *Hitlerjugend* began arriving in position at Lisieux in the middle of the same afternoon but was immediately moved to the west of Caen, which was to be the scene of some of the worst fighting of the campaign.

Here, the teenagers faced the determined Canadian 3rd Division, but were unable to bring their whole strength to bear because half their tanks had been stranded en route from Paris due to lack of fuel. Kurt 'Panzer' Meyer, commander of the 12th SS Panzer Regiment, put the remaining tanks and their supporting infantry into concealed positions behind a low ridge, emphasizing the need to hide their presence until the very last moment. This the eager youngsters of the *Hitlerjugend* did very well, holding their fire until the Canadians were no more than a hundred yards (80 m) away, then advancing full-pelt in a fanatical charge while their anti-tank guns poured fire into the enemy's flanks.

The counter-attack failed to push the invaders

Right *A welcome mug of something hot for a well wrapped-up grenadier* (BPK WII193 F 7184a).

Hitler's Teutonic Knights

Right *PzKpfw III and infantry come under fire, December 1941* (BPK WII139 F 3278c).

Left *A Messerschmitt 110 overflies German tanks on the steppes, summer 1942* (BPK WII147 F 3275b).

Right *StuG IIIs entrained for the front in Russia* (BPK WII216 F 6375b).

Above *PzKpfw III charges across the blazing landscape* (BPK WII153 F 4374).

Below *SS graves outside Kharkov following the bitter fighting of spring 1943* (BPK WII413 F 6412).

back into the sea as intended, but succeeded in preventing their capture of Caen airfield, an important tactical objective. The *Hitlerjugend* had lost six tanks and 200 casualties, but inflicted considerably more damage on its opponents. Next day, 8 June, its second tank battalion (the Panther battalion) finally turned up, and the division went on to the offensive, although its attack quickly bogged down in the face of the intense and demoralizing Allied air attacks. More problems occurred on 16 June, following the collapse of the Panzer Lehr Division on *Hitlerjugend*'s flank, for its beloved commander, Fritz Witt, was killed in his headquarters by either uncannily accurate or lucky naval shell fire. 'Panzer' Meyer assumed his place. For the next fortnight the division fought heroically, tenaciously holding on to the airfield at Le Carpiquet, although it was forced out of the village of the same name. By 9 July, however, it had lost an incredible sixty per cent of its original strength in manpower and only a third of its 150 tanks were left.

Two days later the *Hitlerjugend* was withdrawn, ironically as it turned out, to Falaise. At the end of the month the victorious Americans were pouring into Brittany and around on to the German left flank at St Lô. Then, on 7 August, the Canadians launched a renewed assault. The fifty-odd remaining tanks of the *Hitlerjugend* were faced by *twelve* times their own number. Amazingly, they held out for a full 24 hours before Meyer withdrew them. Day by day their numbers were still further reduced. In one encounter, some sixty men held out for three days in a French schoolhouse against insuperable odds; when they finally ran out of ammunition and surrendered, there were only four survivors. Then came the division's most incredible feat. As described in Chapter 1, some nineteen German divisions, including the remnants of six SS Panzer divisions, were trapped in the 'Falaise Pocket'. There was a narrow exit about 24 miles (38 km) across through which the survivors were pouring as quickly as they could in the face of the devastating air attacks. *Hitlerjugend* was principally responsible for holding open the northern end of this corridor until the flow ceased, the remaining 60,000 men in the pocket being either killed or taken prisoner. But *Hitlerjugend* as a division had practically ceased to exist—only 300 men and ten tanks survived, from an

Left *Line-up of* Hitlerjugend *PzKpfw IVs in Normandy* (BA 297/1740/19a).

Hitler's Teutonic Knights

PzKpfw IVs of the Hitlerjugend Division in France. Painting girlfriends' names on their vehicles seems popular with these young crewmen, several of whom are wearing the black leather U-boat clothing peculiar to this unit (BA 297/1722/23, 24, 26 & 28, 297/1726/17 & 297/1725/37).

Above *Field Marshal von Rundstedt with 'Panzer' Meyer, Fritz Witt and 'Sepp' Dietrich* (BA 297/1739/16a).

Below *Black leather-jacketed* Hitlerjugend *tank commander* (BA 297/1725/9).

Hitler's Teutonic Knights

original strength of 21,300. It was a disaster of the first magnitude for Nazi Germany.

The men of the division had unquestionably fought hard and well. Equally, they rivalled the Leibstandarte and *Das Reich* for barbarity. In the first ten days of their campaign, 64 British and Canadian prisoners of war were murdered—many of them being already wounded. At Nuremberg it was established that some, if not all, of the division's officers had been given orders to kill all prisoners after they had been questioned. 'Panzer' Meyer was convicted of war crimes and sentenced to death. . .a sentence which was commuted in 1954.

After their decimation in Normandy, the remnants of the division retired into Holland, behind the River Maas, and then returned to Germany where they formed the cadre of a resurrected *Hitlerjugend*. This constituted part of Hausser's 6th SS Panzer Army during the Ardennes offensive but, like other units in this assault, was blocked by the appalling road conditions and eventually forced to retreat. It then took part, along with other SS divisions, in the abortive attempt to relieve Budapest, before retreating into Austria and entering American captivity. Proving its fanatical determination, there were only 455 survivors.

Below Hitlerjugend *grenadiers with American prisoners during the Ardennes offensive. The man in the centre carries a Panzerfaust anti-tank missile* (BPK WII116 F 7489).

8. The other 'Panzer' divisions

Apart from the preceding seven premier Waffen-SS Panzer divisions, the following units became Panzergrenadier divisions lacking only a second armoured battalion to qualify themselves for the full title. With the exception of the Polizei Division, which remained a second-rate unit throughout the war, the others fully 'won their spurs' and deserve at least the following brief comments.

4th SS Polizei Panzergrenadier Division

Raised on October 1940 from Ordnungspolizei units, this division was never fully a member of the Waffen-SS, although granted this status in February 1942: its members wore police collar patches and had the police badge on the side of their helmets instead of the SS runes and other insignia. It was formed under the leadership of Gruppenführer Pfeffer-Wildenbruch and, following occupation duties in Poland, saw limited action as a reserve unit in France in 1940. The division's performance alongside that of *Totenkopf* as part of Army Group North in 1941 was indifferent, to say the least, but superior to that of Kampfgruppe *Nord*. In 1943 the division was transferred to the Balkans for anti-partisan duties in Greece and Yugoslavia, where atrocities were committed and the combat record against formed troops poor. At the beginning of 1945 the division was transferred to Poland, where it was engaged in unsurprisingly heavy fighting but acquitted itself well. Some of the survivors fought during the final defence of Berlin and the remainder surrendered to the American Army in May 1945.

7th SS Freiwilligen Gebirgs Division *Prinz Eugen*

A unit with one of the worst records for atrocities, *Prinz Eugen* was raised in March 1942 from ethnic volunteers—mostly Austrian and Rumanian in origin—in the Balkans, and served in this region throughout the war. Surprisingly for a mountain division, it was equipped with tanks although these, like most of the rest of the division's arms, were of obsolete or second-line quality. In 1944-45, while engaged principally against Tito's partisans in Yugoslavia, it encountered heavy fighting against the advancing Soviet Army. Unfortunately for its survivors, the division's last commander, Oberführer Schmidhuber, surrendered to the partisans at Cilli in Slovenia after the German surrender in May 1945, and most were either killed out of hand or executed subsequently for numerous war crimes.

11th SS Freiwilligen Panzergrenadier Division *Nordland*

In the summer of 1943 the *Nordland* Regiment was detached from the *Wiking* Division to form the cadre of a brand-new Germanic division. Originally it included some Dutchmen but they in turn were used to form their own division, *Nederland* (see

Right *Early PzKpfw VAs being photographed by an officer of the 16th SS Panzergrenadier Division in Rome* (BA 716/11/8).

Above *Leon Dégrelle in Army uniform as head of the Walloon Legion from which the 28th SS Panzergrenadier Division evolved* (Christopher Ailsby Photographic Collection).

Above left *Dutch Waffen-SS troops after selection for officer training at Bad Tölz* (Christopher Ailsby Photographic Collection).

Below left *Norwegian volunteers in Russia* (BA 75/120/4a).

below), and *Nordland* became almost entirely Scandinavian, with one regiment of Danes and one of Norwegians (*Danmark* and *Norge*); the division's Panzer Abteilung was called *Hermann von Salza*. After a couple of months' 'working up' in anti-partisan duties in Croatia, the division was sent to Russia where it formed part of Felix Steiner's 3rd (Germanische) Panzer Korps during the extremely heavy fighting on the Baltic coast during 1944. The survivors of this were evacuated by sea from the Courland peninsula to Pomerania and saw further tough action around Danzig before being pulled back to Berlin where the remnants of the division were annihilated.

16th SS Panzergrenadier Division *Reichsführer-SS*

In February 1943 Himmler enlarged his own personal SS escort battalion, the Begleit Bataillon Kommandostab RF-SS, to the size of a brigade. It was stationed on Corsica during the summer of that year then, in October, further enlarged to a division with recruits from Austria and Slovenia. Part of the division was engaged in trying to repel the Allied landing at Anzio while the remainder took part in the occupation of Hungary in March 1944. In May the two halves of the division were reunited in Italy where they fought during the long retreat up the

west coast. In September they were engaged in a reprisal operation against partisans which resulted in the massacre of 2,700 men, women and children at Monte Sol, for which their commander, Max Simon, was later condemned to death. (Once again, the sentence was commuted and Simon was freed in 1954.) The division gradually retreated into Hungary where, with the *Totenkopf*, *Wiking* and other divisions, it took part in the abortive battle to relieve Budapest north of Lake Balaton. The survivors surrendered to American forces at Klagenfurt.

17th SS Panzergrenadier Division *Götz von Berlichingen*

Late in 1943 this division was raised in France under the command of Werner Ostendorff from reserve and training units and brought up to strength with ethnic volunteers from the Balkans. It was continuously involved on the western front from D-Day onwards, participating in the attempt to contain the American breakout at Avranches and subsequently being withdrawn first to Paris and then to Metz. Next it fought in Alsace, being gradually

Various views of 16th SS Panzergrenadier Division StuG IIIs in Italy. The Sigrunes on the gun mantlets appear peculiar to this formation (BA 305/700/6, 11 & 19 & 312/992/13a).

Hitler's Teutonic Knights

forced back into Bavaria where it finally surrendered to US forces near Achensee in May 1945.

18th SS Freiwilligen Panzergrenadier Division *Horst Wessel*

Formed at the beginning of 1944 from Hungarian Germans, it spent most of the year in training and anti-partisan duties. In August one regiment was used in helping to suppress the Slovak uprising while the other fought on the Russian front near Lvov. The two were reunited outside Budapest during the heavy fighting for that city and the division slowly retreated into Czechoslovakia, where it was virtually destroyed.

23rd SS Freiwilligen Panzergrenadier Division *Nederland*

In July 1943 the Freiwilligen Legion *Niederlande* was expanded to the size of a division, many of its personnel coming from the former *Wiking* Division Regiment *Nordland* (see above). Its two regiments were named *General Seyffert* and *De Ruiter*. The division fought alongside *Nordland* on the Baltic front as part of Steiner's 3rd (Germanische) Panzer

Above left *Communications trench of the* Polizei *Division* (BA 694/305/9a).

Below left *Sturmbannführer, possibly of the* Nordland *Division* (BA 77/127/16).

Above *Leon Dégrelle with other survivors from Cherkassy, 8 March 1944* (Archiv Yad Vaschen FA-147 via BPK).

Korps and was also evacuated from Courland. It too fought in Pomerania before being moved back for the final defence of Berlin where it was virtually wiped out, the few survivors surrendering to American troops at Magdeburg. Like their parent division, *Wiking*, both *Nederland* and *Nordland* had extremely high fighting reputations.

28th SS Panzergrenadier Division *Wallonien*

The Belgian fascist leader Léon Dégrelle's Wallonische Legion fought as an Army unit until the middle of 1943, when it was taken into the SS and re-formed as the SS Sturmbrigade *Wallonien*, with Dégrelle himself as its commander. At the end of the year it was operating alongside *Wiking* and was similarly trapped in the Cherkassy pocket; there were some 2,000 survivors at the beginning of the breakout operation—only 632 remained at the end. Withdrawn to Debika in Poland, it was re-formed as a division with recruits from Belgium, France and even Spain. The division fought during the long retreat from Pomerania throughout the spring of 1945. By the end of the war the division had again been reduced to some 700 men, half of whom were captured by the Russians, the remainder surrendering to the British in Denmark. Dégrelle himself made a timely exit and flew to Spain where he received sanctuary.

Superb view of a PzKpfw VA well covered with Zimmerit, also photographed in Italy. No divisional markings are visible but this is possibly a Leibstandarte vehicle (BA 478/2164/27).

Above left *Motor cyclists of a* Totenkopf *reconnaissance unit in Russia* (BA 78/22/7).

Above *Light car clearly showing the* Totenkopf *Division's insignia* (BA 78/22/13).

Left Wiking *Division officers Fritz Vogt, Hans Weiss and Johannes Mühlenkamp* (BA 75/135/36).

Hitler's Teutonic Knights

Above right *Motor cyclists of the* Totenkopf *Division cross a rudimentary bridge* (BA 78/22/14).

Right *Pak 35/36 being towed along the bed of a stream by a truck of the* Totenkopf *Division* (BA 77/93/7).

Above left *Decorations being awarded to men of the* Totenkopf *Division by an SS Untersturmführer. They are smartly dressed in standard field grey uniforms and black marching boots* (BA 78/22/20).

Above right *Grenadier of the* Totenkopf *Division in 1941. His belt buckle identifies him as an officer, rank unknown* (BA 78/22/9).

Opposite page, top *SS reconnaissance unit with an SdKfz 223 in Russia* (BA 73/82/43).

Right Totenkopf *trucks loaded on railway flatbed trucks* (BA 73/83/73).

Left *SS radio operators in Russia.*
Above *The same type of equipment in use by troops in camouflaged smocks, also showing the method of carrying the radio* (Christopher Ailsby Historical Archives).
Below *Reconnaissance unit of the* Reich *division* (BA 81/141/21, 77/93/17 & 18).

Background photograph *SS infantry assault a Soviet strong-point* (BA 209/71/35).

Inset *A battery of sFH 18 howitzers being camouflaged* (BA 209/87/5).

Self-propelled artillery. **Above** *A Wespe.* **Below** *a Marder III with Russian 7.62 mm gun.* **Right** *Very rare photo indeed, and probably taken quite late in the war (1942 at the earliest), of SS tank crewmen and infantry being awarded the Iron Cross 1st Class. (The standard bearer on the right is an officer and appears to have the 25 Class Tank Assault Badge.) What makes this so unusual is the wearing of the black Panzer beret. The double white stripes on the foreground man's sleeves are the silver braid insignia of the 'Spiess', or senior NCO in a unit* (Christopher Ailsby Historical Archives).

Hitler's Teutonic Knights

SS infantryman with standard 98K carbine slung on his back. Note typical style of Russian village architecture in the background (BA 78/22/27).

Waffen-SS grenadiers await a Soviet attack behind a bank. Note the reversible winter camouflage jackets (BA 78/22/4).

Well-muffled SS grenadier during the bitter winter fighting of 1941-42 (BA 78/22/36).

The man on the left wears rubberized motor cycle clothing, while his companions are in standard camouflage smocks (BA 78/22/6).

Hauptscharführer Erich Rech, showing the NCO's rank insignia very clearly (BA 81/113/16a).

Obersturmbannführer Otto Weidinger, who in post-war years has written the definitive history (in German) of the Das Reich *Division (BA 77/93/12).*

SS-Sturman wearing side cap with the camouflaged smock. Note ammunition pouches for his MP38/40 (BA 74/75/40).

Another SS-Sturmann whose equipment includes binoculars, a map case and a stick grenade (BA 77/93/11).

Background photograph *Reich Grenadiers debus, presumably to investigate a Russian sniper in the corn or the bushes.*
Inset *A grenadier replaces a bayonet which has presumably just been used before getting on the pillion of the motor cycle (BA 73/83/62 & 68).*

Left *Useful shot of a PzKpfw III showing the 'sit' of the suspension on uneven ground* (BA 214/349/20a).

Below left *Well-worn whitewash camouflage on an SS PzKpfw III revealing the Panzer grey paint behind the hull crosses and a red numeral 5 on the turret* (Christopher Ailsby Historical Archives).

Below *The crew of a* Das Reich *PzKpfw III pose beside their vehicle during the battle of Kursk* (BA 81/143/14a).

Right *SS Marder III with crew in reversible winter uniforms* (BA 77/127/11).

Above left *SS grenadiers in Kharkov. They are wearing the special SS-issue anoraks which were in great demand* (BA 73/86/63).

Left Das Reich *grenadiers during the street fighting in Kharkov. The foreground figure is carrying a spare barrel and ammunition box for an MG42* (BA 73/84/51).

Above *Pause in the fighting for this group of SS soldiers in Russia* (BA 73/94/16).

Below *Grizzled SS grenadier, believed to belong to the* Wiking *Division, gives advice to some young Army soldiers. The device worn like a 'bleeper' by the man on the right is a field torch* (Christopher Ailsby Historical Archives).

Above left *Although the troops complained about receiving wine instead of ammunition during the winter of 1941, it appears to be more welcome here!* (BA 73/95/14).

Left *Wounded SS grenadier, perhaps indicating what he thinks of the situation!* (BA 73/89/28).

Above *PzKpfw IVs half submerged in the Russian landscape* (BA 216/413/21).

Above right Das Reich *Tiger during 1943 displaying the special Kursk tactical marking* (BA 78/20/1a).

Right *StuG III during the battle of Kursk* (BA 22/2944/2a).

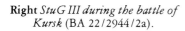

Hitler's Teutonic Knights

A typical scene during the battle of Kursk — SS grenadiers, half-tracks and artillery pieces litter the landscape (BA 81/143/8a).

Left Das Reich *Tigers during the winter of 1943. The white mark on the side of the turret is the 'gnome' device worn by the 8th schwere Panzer Kompanie* (BA 571/1721/29).

Below left *Rear view of two more Tigers of the same unit* (BA 571/1721/32).

Above right *The special Kursk device can still be seen on the hull front of this* Das Reich *Tiger* (BA 571/1721/18).

Right *A Panther photographed at the same time. No divisional markings are apparent* (BA 571/1721/13).

A disabled Tiger, probably photographed during the winter of 1942. This would make a perfect diorama project for military modellers (BA 458/77/16).

Above *PzKpfw V Panther, possibly of the Leibstandarte, in the Flemish town of Diksmuide* (BA 300/1876/4a).

Above centre *Another Panther of the same unit. The name 'Peiper' can just be discerned on one of the signposts* (BA 300/1876/2a).

Above right *The battle of Arnhem — a Marder III moves past the wing of a Horsa glider* (BA 493/3364/19a).

Far right *British wounded in Arnhem alongside an SS StuG III* (BA 497/3527/19a).

Right *PzKpfw IVH. Note white paint used on the interiors of all German tanks until the crews scraped it off — flying paint splinters can be dangerous* (BA 493/3355/24).

Background photograph *Tigers of schwere SS Panzer Abteilung 101 photographed in the vicinity of Rouen, 1944* (BA 299/1804/7).

Inset *SS StuG III in Oosterbeek* (BA 497/3529/6).

Overleaf top *Another view of sSS-PzAbt 101 Tigers in France* (BA 299/1804/15).

Overleaf bottom *Tiger of the 1st Kompanie, sSS-PzAbt 101, in Morgny* (BA 299/1804/4)

Overleaf right *Another vehicle of the same unit drives past a parked Schwimmwagen* (BA 299/1804/6).

179

Left *A letter from home for a Wiking Division Sturmann, eagerly shared by a grenadier and a Panzer Rottenführer (BA 78/2/2).*

Below left *A Leibstandarte PzKpfw IV during the battle for Kharkov in 1943 (BA 75/119/24).*

Above right *Crew of a Leibstandarte PzKpfw IV during the harsh fighting in the Kamenets-Podolsk pocket (BA 689/195/12).*

Right *An early StuG III of the Florian Geyer Division, with two grenadiers from a mortar detachment (BA 73/113/5).*

Hitler's Teutonic Knights

Above left and left *Tiger IIs shelter from the unfriendly eyes of Allied aircraft during the Normandy campaign* (BA 721/359/37 & 721/363/5).
Above and below *Training on Tiger IIs at Sennelager* (BA 721/397/27 & 29).
Below left *The finest tank destroyer of the war, the Jagdpanther mounted a long-barrelled 8.8 cm gun on a Panther chassis* (BA 721/396/14).

Fine view of a Tiger II at Sennelager (BA 721/399/17).

Tiger IIs of schwere Panzer Abteilung 503 Feldherrnhalle *which fought alongside the SS in Budapest in 1945 with (below) an SdKfz 252 ammunition carrier* (BA 680/8282a/3a, 16a & 9a & 84/3416/16).

Feldherrnhalle *Tiger IIs in Budapest, watched by* Totenkopf *grenadiers* (BA 680/8282a/17a, 18a & 38a).

Hitler's Teutonic Knights

Appendices

1. SS Kriegsberichter

Many readers of *Hitler's Samurai* and PSL's earlier 'World War 2 Photo Album' series have asked for additional information about the photographers who took the often marvellous pictures which we have selected for inclusion in the pages of these books. As far as the SS is concerned, I am indebted to Andrew Mollo for the following.

Waffen-SS headquarters authorized the formation of a company of war correspondents in January 1940. Recruits were drawn from obvious newspaper, film and radio commentators and photographers, and the first three sections were allocated to the Leibstandarte, to the SS-VT and to the *Totenkopf* Division prior to the invasion of the west in May 1940. Their early photographs often have a 'family snapshot' air to them and there are few front-line battle shots. In Russia this changed, and the SS-Kriegsberichter showed their mettle by accompanying the points of the advancing columns rather than staying in relative safety with the headquarters units or relying on 'posed' battle scenes, although an element of these continued to be taken throughout the war.

In August 1941, in keeping with the general expansion within the Waffen-SS, the company was enlarged to battalion size, and in December 1943 to that of a regiment. At this time the men in its ranks received new cuff-titles to replace their former SS-KB-Abt or *SS-Kriegsberichter* ones (in either Gothic or Roman script). In honour of one of the battalion's foremost photographers, Kurt Eggers, who had been killed with the *Wiking* Division near Kharkov on 13 August 1943, the following order went out from the SS Führungshauptampt: 'The Führer has awarded the war correspondents units of the Waffen-SS, the name "SS-Standarte Kurt Eggers"'. Thenceforth, the photographers and writers wore a white-on-black armband bearing the name 'Kurt Eggers'. Many continued to wear their old cuff titles simultaneously, and several were also granted the honorary privilege of wearing additionally the armband of the SS regiment or division to which they were attached.

Unfortunately, in the records of the Bundesarchiv or the Preussicher Bildarchiv Kulturbedienst it is usually impossible to identify individual photographers or their achievements, so with one or two exceptions they do not feature in the picture acknowledgements.

2. Composition of an SS Panzer regiment

The following breakdown, which may be taken as typical, is that of the 5th SS Panzer Regiment, *Wiking* Division, in February 1944, and is abstracted from the regiment's own pictorial history *Verweht sind die Spuren*, published by Munin Verlag GmbH of Osnabrück in 1979.

Regimental staff Eight PzKpfw Vs numbered *R00* to *R07;* signals truck; five SdKfz 251 half-tracks or tracked trucks (Maultiers or similar); three flakvier-

Right *A Norwegian SS volunteer with a cine camera. He lacks the normal SS-Kriegsberichter armband (BA 73/89/6).*

lings; seven Kubelwagens; eight Kettenkraftrads; two BMW or Zundapp motor cycle combinations.

1st Battalion Staff company: eight PzKpfw IVs numbered *100* to *107*; trucks, half-tracks, etc, as above. 1st-3rd Panzer companies: seventeen PzKpfw IVs apiece, numbered *111* to *135, 211* to *235* and *311* to *335*, with company headquarters tanks *100, 101, 200, 201, 300* and *301*; 4th Panzer company, seventeen StuG IIIs numbered *411* to *435* plus *400* and *401*. Also, two Kubelwagens and two motor cycle combinations per company.

2nd Battalion As 1st Battalion, but PzKpfw Vs instead of IVs, numbered in the *500, 600, 700* and *800* series, eg, *511* to *535* plus *500* and *501*; also, only one Kubelwagen per company and a Kettenkraftrad instead of the two motor cycles.

Behind these followed a vast array of trucks, half-tracks, engineering and bridging vehicles, workshop trucks, breakdown trucks, a gantry trailer, two tank transporters and numerous trailers, Kubelwagens and motor cycle combinations.

3. SS Panzer division markings

Full divisional markings were more rarely applied to tanks than to half-tracks and 'soft-skin' vehicles; in particular, from photographic evidence, very few PzKpfw V Panthers carried such markings.

Leibstandarte *Adolf Hitler* In 1940 a white key (derived from the divisional commander's name, 'Dietrich' meaing 'key' in German) angled from bottom left to top right, within a plain black shield outline; in 1941 the same but with the shield outline in white; later in the same year, some vehicles began appearing with the key still slanted but the shield

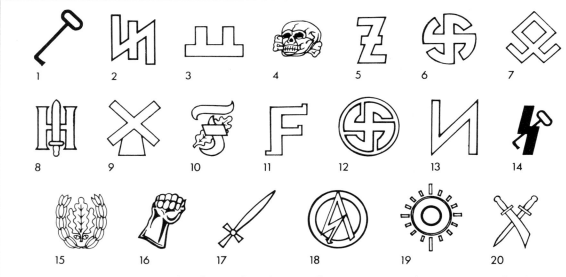

SS Panzer and Panzergrenadier divisional markings. 1 1st SS Panzer Division Leibstandarte Adolf Hitler. **2** *2nd SS Panzer Division* Das Reich. **3** Das Reich *Kursk marking.* **4** *3rd SS Panzer Division* Totenkopf. **5** *4th SS Polizei Panzergrenadier Division.* **6** *5th SS Panzer Division* Wiking. **7** *7th SS Freiwilligen Gebirgs Division* Prinz Eugen. **8** *9th SS Panzer Division* Hohenstaufen. **9** Hohenstaufen *variant, in red, used after Arnhem.* **10** *10th SS Panzer Division* Frundsberg. **11** Frundsberg *variant, white on yellow rhomboid.* **12** *11th SS Freiwilligen Panzergrenadier Division* Nordland. **13** Nordland *variant.* **14** *12th SS Panzer Division* Hitlerjugend. **15** *16th SS Panzergrenadier Division* Reichsführer-SS. **16** *17th SS Panzergrenadier Division* Götz von Berlichingen. **17** *18th SS Freiwilligen Panzergrenadier Division* Horst Wessel. **18** Horst Wessel *variant.* **19** *23rd Freiwilligen Panzergrenadier Division* Nederland. **20** *28th SS Freiwilligen (Panzer) Division* Wallonien. *Drawings by John Major, reproduced from Terence Wise's book* Military Vehicle Markings, *also published by PSL.*

upright, and with a 'notch' taken out of the right-hand corner, as it appears on the cover of this book; in 1942 the shield became rounded at the bottom and was flanked by a white laurel wreath; later this was reduced (1943-45) to a pair of laurel leaves beneath the shield; for Operation 'Zitadelle' a special device was applied—an inverted 'T' in white. Use of these devices overlapped and when one was 'officially' discontinued it was often not repainted for months afterwards, if at all.

Das Reich A letter 'Z' on its side with a central, vertical stroke (*Wolfsangel*), usually painted in yellow but sometimes in white. For Kursk, the special device was the same as the Leibstandarte's except that the 'T' had two vertical bars.

Totenkopf A 'skull and crossbones' in white throughout the war. For Kursk, an inverted 'T' with three vertical bars. The exact shape of the skull and the degree of detail incorporated depended on the artistic skill of the crewman detailed to execute it.

Wiking A 'sun wheel'—a swastika with curved outer bars (see cover of book), in yellow, black or white, sometimes on a black circle; from 1943 it was sometimes seen inside a white outline shield.

Hohenstaufen An upright dagger through a capital letter 'H', in white.

Frundsberg The outline of a Gothic letter 'F' superimposed on a single laurel leaf slanting from left to right with a rhomboid in the centre. Later a simpler capital letter 'F' either in outline, or solid within a rhomboid, appeared.

Hitlerjugend A single Gothic letter 'S' with a Leibstandarte-type key running diagonally through the centre, within a white outline shield above two white outline laurel leaves.

Other markings PzKpfw VI Tiger tanks were not permanently attached to the SS divisions; instead, companies were allocated for specific operations, such as Kursk. These are discussed in full detail in Bruce Culver's *Panzer Colours 3*, published by Squadron/Signal in North America and Arms and Armour Press in the UK. At the battle of Kharkov in February/March 1943, the Leibstandarte had one such company whose vehicles were numbered *411* to *435*; later, at Kursk, their Tigers were numbered *1301* to *1313* and bore, additionally, the special 'inverted ".T"' marking.

During the same operation, *Das Reich*'s Tigers were numbered *S11* to *S14*, *S21* to *S24* and *S31* to *S34*, 'S' standing for 'schwere' (heavy) and the numbering probably being deliberately misleading in the hope that the Russians would think one company was in fact three. *Das Reich* Tigers also carried, in addition to their special Kursk marking, a little white 'gnome' stencilled on their turrets which is evident in some of the photographs in this book.

Totenkopf Tigers were numbered *111* to *124* in the standard way as if they were the 1st Company in the regiment, their commander's tank being number *100*.

In 1944, schwere Panzer Abteilung 101 was formed as the Tiger battalion for 1st SS Panzer Korps in the west, and its tanks bore crossed keys within a shield with flanking oakleaves, reflecting its close links with the Leibstandarte and leading to rumours which have been perpetuated in other books that the Leibstandarte itself was elevated to Korps level. In fact, the battalion fought with *Hitlerjugend*. . . The same markings were carried by the unit after it had been re-equipped with Tiger IIs for the Ardennes offensive, where it operated in the rear of Peiper's Kampfgruppe but achieved nothing.

For tactical markings on tanks and other vehicles, since these were common to both the Army and the Waffen-SS, I would refer readers to the numerous specialized reference books available.

SS-Kriegsberichter in camouflage smock, with cine camera (Christopher Ailsby Historical Archives).

Select bibliography

Beadle, C., and Hartmann, Theodor: *Waffen-SS—Its Divisional Insignia* (Key Publications, 1971).

Bender, R.J., and Taylor, H.P.: *Uniforms, Organisation and History of the Waffen-SS* (four volumes), (Bender-Taylor Publishing, 1969-75).

Buss, Philip H., and Mollo, Andrew: *Hitler's Germanic Legions* (Macdonald and Jane's, 1978).

Butler, Rupert: *The Black Angels* (Hamlyn Paperbacks, 1978).

Culver, Bruce: *Panzer Colours 1-3* (Squadron/Signal, 1976-1984).

Dallin, Alexander: *German Rule in Russia 1941-1945* (Macmillan, 1957).

Davies, Brian Leigh: *Badges and Insignia of the Third Reich* (Blandford, 1983).

Davies, W.K.J.: *German Army Handbook* (Arco, 1984).

Downing, David: *The Devil's Virtuosos: German Generals at war 1940-45* (New English Library, 1977).

Graber, G.S.: *History of the SS* (Robert Hale, 1978).

Hausser, Paul: *Waffen-SS im Einsatz* (Plesse Verlag, 1953).

Höhne, Heinz: *The Order of the Death's Head* (Martin Secker & Warburg, 1969).

Holzmann, Walther-Karl: *Manual of the Waffen-SS* (Argus, 1976).

Infield, Glenn B.: *Secrets of the SS* (Stein & Day, 1982).

Keegan, John: *Waffen SS: the asphalt soldiers* (Ballantine, 1970).

Lefèvre, Eric: *Panzers in Normandy Then and Now* (After the Battle, 1983).

Littlejohn, David: *Foreign Legions of the Third Reich* (four volumes) (Bender-Taylor Publishing).

Lucas, James, and Cooper, Matthew: *Hitler's Elite: Leibstandarte SS 1933-45* (Macdonald and Jane's, 1975).

Mitcham, Samuel W.: *Hitler's Legions* (Leo Cooper, 1985).

Mollo, Andrew: *A Pictorial History of the SS 1923-1945* (Macdonald and Jane's, 1976); *Waffen-SS Badges and Unit Distinctions* (Historical Research Unit, 7 volumes, 1970s).

Perrett, Bryan: *Lightning War* (Panther, 1985).

Reitlinger, Gerald R: *The SS: Alibi of a Nation 1922-1945* (Heinemann, 1956).

Richardson, William and Freidin, Seymour: *The Fatal Decisions* (Consul, 1965).

Schneider, Jost W.: *Their Honour Was Loyalty* (R. James Bender Publishing, 1977).

Stein, George H.: *The Waffen SS: Hitler's élite guard at war 1939-45* (Cornell University Press, 1966).

Stern, Robert C.: *SS Armour: A pictorial history of the armoured formations of the Waffen-SS* (Squadron/Signal, 1978).

Verweht sind die Spuren (Munin Verlag, 1979).

Wenn Alle Brüder Schweigen (Munin Verlag, 1973).

Windrow, Martin: *Waffen SS* (Osprey, 1971), and: *The Waffen SS* (revised edition) (Osprey, 1982).

Notes and acknowledgements

The photographs in this book come predominantly from the Bundesarchiv, Koblenz, and are credited 'BA' followed by the negative reference number at the end of each caption. As Patrick Stephens Limited have explained in previous books using photographs from this source, the Bundesarchiv pictures are only available to *bona fide* authors and publishers, not to private collectors and enthusiasts. The Bundesarchiv simply do not have the resources to cope with the volume of demand which would otherwise result. We hope readers will appreciate that this situation is not of our making and that for similar reasons we cannot supply copy prints of photographs in this book.

Some readers will find several of the Bundesarchiv photographs familiar because they have previously been published — usually for the first time — in Patrick Stephens' earlier *World War 2 Photo Album* series, which is now out of print. In many cases these have been repeated here because subsequent information has come to light identifying individuals, locations or dates more precisely, or correcting earlier errors in captioning. I would particularly like to thank: Frank R. Beattie, Josef Charita, A. G. Dixon, L. Ferdinand-Fricke, J. Freitas, Kenneth M. Jones, Jean-Pierre Petit, Timo Tuominen, Andrew Willis and Fernando J. De Zavala.

Other photographs, also acknowledged after their captions, come from the Preussicher Bidldarchiv Kulturbedienst in Berlin (credited 'PBK'), including all the colour transparencies. These archives *are* open to students and private researchers.

In preparing this revised edition I am particularly indebted to Mr C. Boland for his helpful comments and constructive criticism.

Final mention must be made of Christopher Ailsby, whose help and advice have been immeasurable, and of Sue Forster for her considerate editing.

Index